About this book

Why is this topic important?

Much is written about *user interface* design. You learn when to click and double-click gestures, how to allow users to sort lists, how to provide a clear screen layout, and so forth. And much is written about *instructional* design: how to write instructional objectives; when to use drill-and-practice, tutorials, and simulations; how to use text and narration; and so forth. But little is written specifically about how to bring it all together to create fantastic e-learning experiences. This needed synthesis is *learner interface* design—the topic of this book.

What can you achieve with this book?

This book will help you use your time and resources effectively to build the best e-learning experiences possible within your constraints. As with the other books in this series, this book is geared toward pragmatic application. It's direct and to the point: here's how to connect with your learners, how to empower learners to make the most of e-learning's capabilities, and how to orchestrate learning events for maximum impact: CEO—connect, empower, and orchestrate.

How is this book organized?

This book is divided into four parts. Part I describes the importance of excellent learner interface. Part II describes learner interface guidelines based on the CEO model: connect, empower, and orchestrate. Part III reviews common mistakes and provides guidelines to assist in focusing on the right things. Part IV provides examples of successful e-learning interfaces. The book also includes a series of challenge exercises and a reference guide of user interface design guidelines.

About the library series

After success with Authorware, Inc., and Macromedia, I felt that I had made a contribution to learning that would satisfy me through retirement. And retire Mary Ann and I did . . . for a few months.

But as my colleagues and I observed what happened with tools that made development of interactive learning systems so much easier to master, it was clear my job wasn't done. Instead of wondrously varied instructional paradigms burgeoning forth, offering more learning fun and effectiveness to the benefit of people and organizations everywhere, we found dry, boring, pedantic presentation of content followed by post-tests. The very model of instruction that was drudgery without technology was being replicated and inflicted on ever-greater numbers of captive audiences.

Making technology easier to use provided the means, but not the guidance, necessary to use it well. To atone for this gross oversight on my part, I formed Allen Interactions in 1993 with a few of my closest and most talented friends in e-learning. Our mission was and is to help everyone and anyone produce better technology-enhanced learning experiences. We established multiple studios within our company so that these teams of artisans could build long-term relationships with each other and their clients. Studios develop great internal efficiencies and, most importantly, get to understand their clients' organizations and performance needs intimately—sometimes better than clients understand them themselves.

Although our studios compete in the custom development arena, we also share our best practices openly and freely. We exhibit our applications as openly as clients allow, hoping they will stimulate critique and discussion so we can all do better and so that successful ideas can be broadly applied. We teach and mentor in-house organizations that aspire to create great learning applications. And, in close association with the American Society for Training and Development (ASTD), we offer certificate programs to help participants develop effective design and development skills.

This series of books is another way we are doing our best to help advance the field of technology-enhanced learning. I've not intentionally held back any secrets in putting forth the best practices our studios are continually enhancing.

This, the third book in the series, presents a lacking and needed synthesis of user interface (UI) design principles used generally in software applications and of specific interface needs required by learning events. Learner interface and UI conflict at times, and learner interface must take precedence over UI in these cases. We expose in this book a number of sources of design influence that authors must be particularly wary of, as they frequently nullify learning impact.

Six books are planned for this library, each to be focused on one major aspect of the process of designing and developing great e-learning applications. When the series is compiled, I hope it will be a useful tool for developing great and valuable learning experiences.

Michael Allen's e-Learning Library

Volume 1	Creating Successful e-Learning— A Rapid System for Getting It Right First Time, Every Time
Volume 2	Designing Successful e-Learning— Forget What You Know About Instructional Design and Do Something Interesting
Volume 3	**Successful e-Learning Interface— Making Learning Technology Polite, Effective, and Fun**
Volume 5	Managing e-Learning Development— Creating Dramatic Successes Even with Outrageous Timelines, Budgets, and Expectations
Volume 4	Deploying e-Learning Successfully— Improving Performance Takes More Than Good Instruction
Volume 6	Evaluating e-Learning Success— Making Evaluation Inexpensive and e-Learning Priceless

Michael Allen's e-Learning Library

Successful e-Learning Interface

Making Learning Technology Polite, Effective, and Fun

Michael W. Allen

Pfeiffer

A Wiley Imprint

www.pfeiffer.com

Published by Pfeiffer
An Imprint of Wiley
989 Market Street, San Francisco, CA 94103-1741
www.pfeiffer.com

For additional copies/bulk purchases of this book in the U.S. please contact 800-274-4434.
Pfeiffer books and products are available through most bookstores. To contact Pfeiffer directly call our Customer Care Department within the U.S. at 800-274-4434, outside the U.S. at 317-572-3985, fax 317-572-4002, or visit www.pfeiffer.com.

Pfeiffer also publishes its books in a variety of electronic formats. Some content that appears in print may not be available in electronic books.

Library of Congress Cataloging-in-Publication Data

Allen, Michael W.
  Michael Allen's e-learning library : successful e-learning interface : making learning technology polite, effective, and fun / Michael W. Allen.
      p. cm.
  Includes index.
  ISBN 978-0-7879-8297-3 (pbk.); ISBN 978-1-118-03467-5 (ebk); ISBN 978-1-118-03684-6 (ebk); ISBN 978-1-118-03685-3 (ebk)
  1. Instructional systems--Design. 2. Educational technology. 3. User interfaces (Computer systems) I. Title.
  LB1028.38.A46 2011
  371.3--dc22
2010048923

Printing 10 9 8 7 6 5 4 3 2 1
Cover photo of Michael Allen by Courtney Platt, Grand Cayman, B.W.I.

Contents

Acknowledgments

An attempt at synthesis and the generation of specific guidelines requires a broad spectrum of knowledge and even broader practical experience. So many principles that seem unarguably right prove to be deceptively damaging propositions in practice. I am particularly grateful to David Conner who, although his comments delayed me almost a full year, read my first draft and pointed out a huge discrepancy. He noted that, while I took pains to differentiate user interface from learner interface, I had then gone on to dwell almost entirely on user interface. That subject, he noted, had already been covered and did not need to be covered again. So I started over, aided by a considerable amount of work on his part to put me on the right path.

Later on, drawing from their rich and extensive experience in the field of e-learning, I was incomparably guided by Ethan Edwards, Paul Howe, Alex Watson, and Richard Sites. Marty Lipshutz, Nicole Wilder, Fred McGrath, and Michelle-Noelle Magallanez joined in as readers and very constructive critics. Ryan Smith, Steve Lee, Peter Lisowski, and Mary-Scott Hunter assisted the others and me with the challenging task of finding examples and obtaining permission to show them. Thanks to Teaching Strategies, Inc., Commission on Peace Officer Standards and Training (POST), Cooliris, Inc., Council on International Educational Exchange, Inc. (CIEE), DaimlerChrysler Corporation, Essilor of America, Inc., Expedia, Inc., Genesco, Inc., HSBC Holdings, PLC, Motorola, Inc., Mr. Wizard Studios, and Twin Cities Public Television, Inc.

So many exemplary projects fail to inspire and guide our field because their owners will not allow them to be seen publicly. I realize that e-learning done well is a treasured competitive advantage, but there is so much to be learned from sharing examples. So again, thanks very much to these organizations and the others who preferred not to be named, even though they allowed me to use snippets of their applications.

Special thanks to Amy Pahl, who coordinated everything and never lost her patience through endless interruptions imposed by other demands for my time and attention. Also thanks to Brendan Stern and Chris Palm for their graphic and layout expertise. And as always, special thanks to Nancy Olson at ASTD for her unfailing enthusiasm for developing this material and coordinating certificate programs based on it.

And finally, once again, I'm searching for words to adequately express appreciation for my family, whose support, tolerance, and encouragement are of greatest importance for the completion of each book. There are no adequate words, but thank you nonetheless. I do hope our combined contributions to these books result in better learning experiences and that those learning experiences lead to more fulfilling and happier lives somewhere, sometime, someplace.

For Ethan Edwards, with whom I've had the pleasure
of working for many years. He has become perhaps the
most trusted and credible industry spokesperson for
quality e-learning experiences. Ethan's creativity, insights,
communication skills, and sense of humor continue to inspire
me and our colleagues every day.

Foreword

"Design is not just what it looks like and feels like. Design is how it works."
—Steve Jobs, CEO, Apple

Steve Jobs' approach has tremendous application for the learning and development field. For learning to be most effective, the design of a course is as important as the content itself. In this third book in his e-learning library series, Michael Allen explains a critical difference between user interface design—the ease and usability of a course—and learner interface design, a focus on helping learners think, learn, and perform. This distinction provides an enlightening perspective for everyone in the field responsible for designing learning.

Throughout the book, Michael provides examples, models, and resources to illuminate the principles of a learner-centric approach to design. One of the approaches that Michael carries through this e-learning series is called the three Ms, and it is an extremely practical model for how we should approach the design of any kind of learning experience:

M1: Is it **meaningful**? Ask yourself: Will learners understand what they are being taught?

M2: Is it **memorable**? Ask yourself: Will they remember what they learned?

M3: Is it **motivational**? Ask yourself: Will learners be motivated to apply their learning?

Another relevant concept is the "CEO" approach: connect, empower, and orchestrate. As Michael describes them, "successful learning experiences connect with learners; empower them to explore, experiment, and react; and orchestrate the learning environment such that it provides critical feedback, help, and guidance." How many of us had a great teacher in our past who was passionate about the subject, encouraged us to be excited, showed us how to apply what we learned, and helped us achieve success? He explains how we can apply this in design using the CEO concepts:

CONNECT: Connecting with learners is more than engaging them in the content and developing their skills; it's also about inspiration, passion, and making the learning a personally rewarding experience.

EMPOWER: Learning comes so easily from doing things first-hand, so e-learning needs to provide both a transparent user interface and an effective learner interface that allows learners to do things (not just flip pages). ORCHESTRATE: Experiences arise from an orchestration of multiple components, including input and control, help and direction, and consequences and feedback. Learner interface is the means of orchestrating these components for the purpose of skill development.

For those readers who like to know the key takeaways for each chapter right up-front, Michael provides those in a section at the beginning called Rapid Reader. These key concepts communicate what I consider to be the "bottom line" for each chapter. For example, the takeaways for Chapter 1 are:

➤ User interface design is about efficiency. Don't make me think.

➤ Learner interface design is about making people think, learn, and perform.
➤ Context is the foundation for interactive learning.

I encourage you to share this book with your colleagues and team members, and make sure the concepts contained in it are part of your design process.

Like all of Michael's books, I know you will find *Successful e-Learning Interface* thought-provoking and engaging and full of practical examples and guidelines to build effective learning experiences. Best wishes for success in your e-learning journey!

Tony Bingham
President and CEO
American Society for
Training and Development
www.astd.org

Preface

This library of books is intended to study selected topics of *Michael Allen's Guide to e-Learning* in more detail than that core, overview book could possibly provide and to offer practical, specific guidelines for successful application. New thoughts, perspectives, and concepts were not expected or particularly welcome.

But just as great ideas tend to emerge at inconvenient times in e-learning application design and development (too late), some great ideas surfaced when my critical readers reviewed the first and second drafts of this book. These ideas led to my chucking the first drafts and starting over, centering, in fact, on these new ideas.

The first two drafts were actually based on a chapter that was omitted from the Guide because the publisher wanted to shorten the book to keep the price as low as possible. It was the right choice. But an important chapter on user interface design was omitted. You know, like avoiding red text on a blue background, providing intuitive ways for learners to order the steps of a sequence, and so on.

What I noted therein was the difference between user interface design (UID) and learner interface design (LID). While UID attempts to minimize the thinking necessary to interact with software, LID works to stimulate the learner's thinking about the subject and skills being learned. UID guidelines present ways to make correct actions obvious to anyone, while LID guidelines present ways to avoid making correct actions obvious to anyone who lacks prerequisite knowledge or skills. UID emphasizes ease of use, while LID emphasizes making the process and learner level of effort commensurate with those that will be used and needed when actually performing learned tasks.

I declared the difference between UID and LID in the first drafts, but my critics pointed out that I devoted nearly all the book to UID topics. There are many excellent books on UID (I happen to particularly like and recommend Scott and Neil's *Designing Web Interfaces* and Buxton's *Sketching User Experiences*), but my readers pointed to the scarcity of credible LID guidelines. They noted their skepticism of research- or "evidence-based" guidelines, because they are so often over-generalized, given too much credence, and lead designers to dogmatically apply and defend principles that don't fit the salient conditions. They wanted guidelines that can truly be trusted. They wanted suggestions for dealing with a wide variety of learners and content. They wanted examples from real-world successes.

So the book before you addresses LID much more than it addresses UID, although a UID guide redux survives in Chapter 8. The other chapters look at LID, using the structural foundations of interactive learning experiences—context, challenge, activity, and feedback—as organizers for the itemized and rather specific guidelines that have been effective in applications across significant varieties of content, time and time again. Chapter 9 provides a compendium of examples.

As always, it's my hope that this material will prove helpful in your efforts to design, build, and provide outstanding learning experiences that help learners realize more of their potential. We continue to find better and easier ways to create such learning experiences, so the guidelines enumerated in this book are (as are all others) subject to continuing evolution. But I have no doubt that if you and I abide by these guidelines, our e-learning will be very successful.

January 15, 2011
MWA

Part One

The Need for Learner Interface Design Excellence

User Interface vs. Learner Interface

Instructional design and *user design* have much in common, but there are areas in which they not only differ, but are also in conflict. What are they, how do they relate, and how can they guide e-learning designers?

Perhaps I can create a small learning experience here that will be meaningful and memorable. Even without my having attempted to define and contrast user interface and learner interface, let's see if you won't get a sense of what each is and why their differences are important by taking a look at a few screen designs and describing what you see. I'll make some notes on the *user interface.* You make notes on the *learner interface* as prompted by the headings.

Challenge 1

The first screen presents content from antiterrorism training and describes four primary principles first responders should use to both keep themselves safe and provide the fastest and best protective reaction.

As a first responder to an incident, remember that you may personally be at risk.

Continue to keep these strategies in mind:

RECOGNIZE: Assess from a safe distance; scan for secondary devices.

AVOID: Stay clear of the danger area. Your own safety comes first.

ISOLATE: Clear the area; establish a perimeter.

NOTIFY: Notify dispatch of all important information; request appropriate personnel; advise others of danger spots.

NEXT

Figure courtesy of Commission on Peace Officer Standards and Training

User Interface Design (UID)

⊙ Successful   ○ Poor

Why? From a user interface perspective, there's little functionality on the screen—few problems, not a lot to go wrong. The forward-paging NEXT button is clear. Considering the layout, the page is nicely organized, key words stand out, and there are generally no issues.

Learner Interface Design (LID)

(Your turn):
○ Successful   ○ Poor

Why?

Context

○ Successful   ○ Poor

Why?

Challenge

O Successful   O Poor

Why?

Activity

O Successful   O Poor

Why?

Feedback

O Successful   O Poor

Why?

Compare and Contrast UI and LID

What works for one, but not the other?

Challenge 2

This design presents the pre-scribed actions, as did Challenge 1, but not in the correct order. The learner has to think about what might be the best order in which to respond to the situation.

As a first responder to an incident, you should first:

○ **ISOLATE:** Clear the area; establish a perimeter.

○ **RECOGNIZE:** Assess from a safe distance; scan for secondary devices.

○ **AVOID:** Stay clear of the danger area. Your own safety comes first.

○ **NOTIFY:** Notify dispatch of all important information; request appropriate personnel; advise others of danger spots.

SUBMIT

This is the feedback that is shown if "AVOID" is chosen and is typical of other feedback messages in this design.

While you'll have to avoid dangerous areas, to do so, you need to determine where the dangers are.

Select another answer.

User Interface Design (UID)

⊙ Successful   ○ Poor

Why? As in Screen 1, there's little functionality on the screen—few problems, not a lot to go wrong. The radio buttons are a standardized and widely recognized interface device. The context and question clearly imply that only one choice can be selected. Instructions could have been added, but probably aren't needed. A rollover highlight (as shown) invites the user to click the button. Such invitations confirm expectations and contribute significantly to user comfort and confidence. Because only one answer can be selected, users can correct errors by simply clicking a preferred answer after making a mistake. The visible SUBMIT button confirms the ability to make corrections but appears inactive, as it should, until an answer is selected. The page is nicely organized, key words stand out, the text is large enough, and it contrasts well. There are generally no significant UI issues.

Learner Interface Design (LID)

○ Successful   ○ Poor

Why?

Context

○ Successful   ○ Poor

Why?

Challenge

○ Successful   ○ Poor

Why?

Activity

○ Successful   ○ Poor

Why?

Feedback

○ Successful   ○ Poor

Why?

Compare and Contrast UI and LID

What works for one, but not the other?

Challenge 3

This screen presents an incident. "An explosion has been reported at 5th and Center Streets. Possible injuries. No further details are available at this time." Learners play the role of first responders and indicate what they would do by clicking the buttons below the scene.

Buttons present more detailed options or ask for further information. A clock times learner responses.

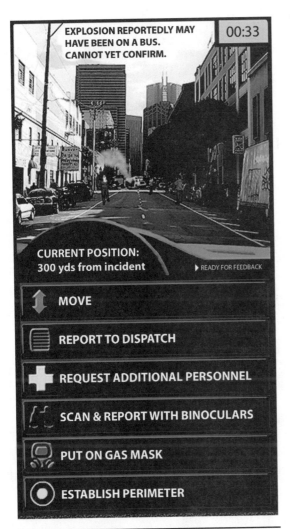

Screen capture courtesy of Commission on Peace Officer Standards and Training

User Interface Design (UID)

⊙ Successful   ○ Poor

Why? This is a much more complex screen, but options that are alternatives to each other are apparent. The situation is described at the top, in the brightest area of the screen, which gets my attention.

Although the clock counting elapsed time at the top is not explained, it's quite clear that it's timing my actions, and I need to avoid wasting time.

The READY FOR FEEDBACK button is related in color and shape to the primary options and communicates that I may want to do more than one thing before I indicate that I'm done. Because it appears active, it needs to be active. It could give some instruction to a user who didn't understand the implications of this screen layout and clicked this button without taking any prior actions.

Overall, this design is working.

Learner Interface Design (LID)

O Successful   O Poor

Why?

Context

O Successful   O Poor

Why?

Challenge

O Successful   O Poor

Why?

Activity

O Successful   O Poor

Why?

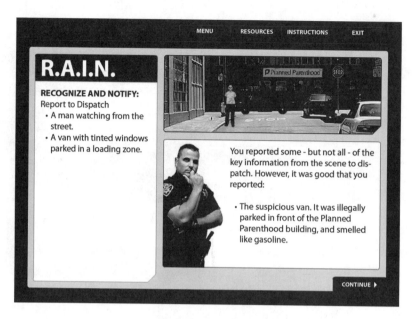

Feedback

O Successful   O Poor

Why?

Compare and Contrast UI and LID

What works for one, but not the other?

1 | Design Magic

I don't know about you, but good interface designs fascinate me. Good interfaces energize me and make me feel a bit more powerful because with them I am more powerful. I can do more, discover more, and achieve more with less effort. Sometimes designs, although no more efficient than others, are just amusing or creative enough to justify their break with conventions and set new expectations. I like that, too. Sometimes interface designs tell me what I need to think about before it would otherwise have occurred to me. Such hints can prompt as much learning as any other component in e-learning. Excellent!

I discovered Cooliris a while ago. As you may know, Cooliris quickly and dramatically creates a visual wall from a pile of images. The company calls it an "infinite 3D wall" that lets you browse content without clicking page to page. Drag its scrollbar and you'll discover an amazingly rapid means of reviewing a very large amount of data in a quick and fascinating way that's hard to describe. When you drag quickly, the wall slants away from you to provide a means of seeing a larger number of images to scan. As you slow down, the wall confronts you straight on. Fewer images are now in view, but they are larger and clearer. Press the space bar to see the center image enlarged, use the arrow keys to select neighboring images, or drag the scroll bar at various speeds forward and back to scan as you wish.

Use it with Google image search, for example, and you'll get an instant sense of how many images matched your search criteria and what the range of styles and items is. The very question that's in your head, *"I wonder what's out there,"* will be answered with instant clarity. You'll want to do more searches just because of the power you have and the pleasantness of the experience.

In the time between my writing and the publication of this book, Cooliris will undoubtedly have evolved. Others will see alternatives and shoot out competing designs. Variations on this theme exist already.

Ɑapid readeɌ

- User interface design is about efficiency. Don't make me think.

- Learner interface design is about making people think, learn, and perform.

- Context is the foundation for interactive learning.

13

Screen capture
courtesy of
Cooliris, Inc.

When someone has broken through a conceptual barrier, cool things frequently spawn a whole family of forward-stepping inventions.

A variant of Cooliris is Apple's Safari Web browser.

This is what design magic is all about. It's as fun as it is useful.

Good user interface designs enable computers to assume an effective and, hopefully, a desirable role in our lives. They take the raw power of computers and networks and turn it into services we can use and appreciate. They can elevate the quality of our lives by helping us make more productive use of precious time, be creative, find and access information when it's needed, and communicate more effectively and expressively with each other. When done well, interface designs adapt computer power to our needs. When done poorly, interface designs require users to adapt to them, reset expectations, and sometimes even combat entrenched behavior patterns to avoid errors.

The Big Message

The big message is this: e-learning needs good user interface design to work. We can little afford to have attention and focus whittled down by confusion and frustration with the mechanics of using a computer. Even without such distractions, we designers are challenged to keep learner attention and focus, without which learning experiences fail.

Even with excellent design, computers exact a price. Learners have to express themselves through the limited gestures the hardware perceives and the software understands. Tomorrow's computers, of course, will recognize more gestures than simply keyboard and mouse inputs. My laptop now recognizes both touch and stylus input directly to the screen. It also has a video camera that can see me, but the software doesn't yet have facial recognition features to scoot me around password-protected identity barriers (although my finger-print reader does sometimes). I don't yet have capabilities for multi-touch input, yet alone for recognizing hand or facial gestures (but I expect to see them in my lifetime). In short, the limited vocabulary of today's usable gestures significantly limits the things learners can do under the mentorship of software. This is an unfortunate penalty of using technology that otherwise has so many advantages.

Since e-learning events must often be used on devices of various configurations, assorted gesture recognition limitations are even more constraining. We have to work with capabilities common to all delivery devices we might need to use. Those common capabilities are typically lower-end capabilities that use less computer power but demand a bit more of the learner's attention—a demand that is easily inflated by poor design. Our designs therefore have a lot to overcome and achieve.

Learner Interface vs. User Interface

Yet another set of challenges exists for us as learning application designers: How do we make learning experiences meaningful, memorable, and motivational? This is where learner interface differs from general user interface issues. While generally all interface designers want to make things easier for users, they often don't care about making their transactions meaningful or memorable. They don't always work to make the user ponder the outcomes of alternative actions. They generally want to minimize mental involvement entirely and may even reward haphazard clicking.

In contrast, learning interface designers must get learners to engage their mental faculties in order to learn. Unlike many design principles appropriate for transactional Web sites, where the goal is challenge-free entry and retrieval of data, e-learning need to confront learners with challenges. Note the differences in the instructions (left) related to the same interaction (right):

Alternative Instructions	Interaction
User Interface Design Click c for information about the true statement. Click misconceptions a, b, and d for related information.	**Plexiglas** a) is heavier than glass b) is toxic, being made from poisonous hydrocyanic acid c) coalesces with human tissues d) is less transparent than typical window glass
Learner Interface Design Think carefully about Plexiglas, a synthetic "organic glass," and click the statement you think is correct.	

Design Goals

Our goals, as learner interface designers, are therefore two-fold: (1) overcoming some negative aspects of using computers for learning and (2) taking full advantage of the benefits and opportunities computer technology affords. The difference between user interface design (UID) and learner interface design (LID) needs to be clear.

1. The **user interface** designer's challenge: Minimize the attention and effort learners must sacrifice in operating the user interface

2. The **learner interface** designer's challenge: Maximize the impact of the learning experience

1. Minimizing the Negative

Humans are adaptable, capable of continuous learning, and yet also resistant to change. Learning is work. It's a disruptive process. It's a change process. Perhaps the reason change is so difficult is literally our physiology. The brain tends to defend itself against assaults to the status quo and it literally heats up, especially when challenges are great. While we are wired to learn, we also have a constitution that prefers familiarity and consistency. This internal battle is escalated when it's clear that the targeted outcome of a learning experience is a change in behavior, where the discomfort of rearranging and augmenting what one knows is accompanied by the risks of actually doing things differently. Mistakes, embarrassment, humiliation, and who knows what are among the potential outcomes.

With all this stirring their minds, we must nevertheless help learners to focus their full energy and concentration to reach successful outcomes. We want them to set aside fears and self-doubts like, *I'm no good at math, I've never been able to sell anything,* and concentrate for the period of time necessary to learn and acquire

17

new skills. And, oh yes, we want them to be working with unfamiliar software under the direction of perhaps the least empathetic of all instructors—a computer.

With all these challenges, we obviously don't want learners inadvertently pressing wrong buttons, being confused about how to correct entries, concerned that getting help will "go on record," mistaking *NEXT* for *SUBMIT*, and so on. The negative aspects of learning via technology must be minimized as much as possible. And this is not a small challenge.

2. Maximizing the Positive

Did you see a *Star Wars* movie? How long ago was that? Like it or hate it, chances are you still remember a very large number of things about it. Costumes, spaceships, animal-

like war machines, English-speaking alien creatures, lightsabers, a guy in a black full-face helmet whose breathing you could hear, *May the Force be with you.* Nodding? I could list plenty more.

You probably can even recall names. Does Princess Leia ring a bell? Luke Skywalker? Chewbacca? Han Solo? How about R2-D2 and C-3PO? I'll bet you could identify them all in a lineup.

Can you list a similar number of things you remember from your last training course? How about the instructor's name? And how long ago was that course?

Now it's certainly possible that the *Star Wars* saga hasn't stuck with you (Who are you?) or that you do actually remember vividly your last instructor's name and what you learned, but I'm sure you get my point. If experiences have a certain dynamic to them, they stick with us much longer than those that are routine. Most training, including most e-learning, is routine at best and, just like a boring movie, it's quickly forgotten.

As stressed in the other books in this series, the operative criteria for e-learning or any learning experience are the three M's:

M1. Is it **meaningful**? If learners don't understand what they're being taught, it will not be helpful to them. It will not improve their performance nor add to their skill sets.

M2. Is it **memorable**? If learners can't remember what they learned, they might as well never have learned it. How can forgotten principles or procedures improve performance?

M3. Is it **motivational**? If learners are not motivated to apply their learning, to rehearse and keep it alive, it will fade. The learning might just as well not have happened.

The *Star Wars* series achieved one of the criteria (memorable) through ways we can understand and articulate to some degree, and that is a major achievement. Their stories include conflict, the drama of human relationships, and discussions of morality, losses, and triumphs. For some viewers, the stories, upstaged as they often were by the special effects, may have provided meaningful and motivational experiences as well. Unfortunately, in training, achieving only one of the three M's is a failure. We must achieve all three and on, I suspect, a somewhat smaller budget than George Lucas had.

Interfacing the Mind

When talking about learner interface design, you might think we were simply addressing the mechanics of interaction—almost as if we were talking only to the fingers. We do, indeed, want gestures to be so automatic that one doesn't have to be cognizant of translating decisions into hand and finger movements. But with learner interface design we're, more importantly, talking about ways to get the mind to exercise productive and useful thought patterns—and then automatically translate them into recognizable gestures for our appraisal.

When thinking of interactions constructed to engage the mind, we turn to CCAF—the four interlocking pieces of the instructional inter-

activity puzzle—context, challenge, activity, and feedback. Of these, context is the foundation and critical to do right before building the others on it.

Throughout this book, we'll be stressing the importance of *context* as the key to orienting and focusing the mind. *Challenges* waken the mind and more fully energize it. *Activity* calls on all the general principles of good user interface design, but contributes effectively only if it relates fully to the context. And finally, as we shall see from examples, *feedback* achieves its greatest effectiveness if, as with the other components, it plays off the context.

2 | Introducing the CEO of LID

"Emily, you're looking like a bright and creative 10-year-old today. So I've got a challenge for you. Show me how to balance a nail, two forks, and a cork all on the end of a pencil. Can you balance them all together while you walk around the room?"

For fifteen years on black-and-white TV, Mr. Wizard challenged "neighborhood" kids in a way that even passive viewers of all ages felt engaged. Those of us who knew what was going to happen when the child aligned magnets backward, put a hardboiled egg over the mouth of a jar containing a burning candle, or reversed DC current to an electric motor couldn't wait to see the child's face when it happened. Children ran to their parents with pleas to try such "science" at home.

Learner interface design (LID) is challenging. As a learner interface designer, you need to interest your learners and maintain that interest. You need to focus learners on what's important and convey information efficiently. You need to provide the means for learner input and control for interactions "that actively stimulate the learner's mind to do those things that improve ability and readiness to perform effectively" (Allen, 2003, p. 255). You need to balance your judgment of how learners can best spend their time and energy against their desires to be in control and exercise their own judgment. You have to create experiences that are instructive, provide sufficient practice, and adapt to individual needs. You have to relate helpful information, such as progress, level of performance, and where additional resources can be found.

Fully enumerated, learner interface design sounds like an intimidating task, but e-learning cannot succeed without good LID. So the question is: How can one go about LID with the best prospects for success?

Let the CEO Take Charge. Connect, Empower, and Orchestrate

Photograph courtesy of Mr. Wizard Studios, Inc.

Successful learning experiences, whether taking advantage of e-learning technology for delivery or not, connect with learners; empower them to explore, experiment, and

react; and orchestrate the learning environment such that it provides critical feedback, help, and guidance.

Over millennia, great teachers have demonstrated their CEO skills in connecting with their students, empowering them to learn, and orchestrating experiences that have benefited their students for the rest of their lives. Don Herbert as the immortal Mr. Wizard mesmerized kids with "the wonders of science" in his TV show that ran from 1951 to 1965, with later revivals. Play some YouTube snippets to see for yourself. Exemplified by Don, great teachers reveal their passion for teaching by finding the fascination in their content matter and building on it. Often with dramatic approaches, they empower their learners to experience the value of new knowledge through exercises that reward learners with success—sometimes successes they never expected to have.

You can do this, too. With the concepts of connecting, empowering, and organizing to prompt and guide you, you can create LIDs with incredible impact. Let me introduce these concepts very briefly here. We'll pick them up in greater detail with examples in later chapters.

C Is for Connect

It's essential to get learners involved, engaged, thinking, and doing things. While general user interface design aspires to transparency and ease of use (*Don't make me think!*), LID aims for just the opposite: *thinking!* While general user interface designs try to minimize the things users need to do to get what they want, LID again aims for just the opposite: getting learners busy doing things— *all the necessary things in real-world tasks*—and doing them repeatedly until strong skills and confidence develop.

But to fully engage learners, we don't just need to connect with our learners' cognitive, perceptive, and motor skills. We need an emotional or affective connection as well. We want learners to not only know how to work the interface mechanisms we provide, but we also want them eager to explore and use these helpful learning affordances to their advantage. We want learners to be enthusiastic both about learning and about eventually applying their learning for meaningful benefits.

As we discussed extensively in the second book of this series, *Designing Successful e-Learning*, instruction and learning are all about achieving behavioral change. We learn things so that we can perform new tasks or improve our skills. We know things so we can do things. But even though the awesome human brain is capable of incredible learning, it also tends to resist change.

Cradled in the comfort of familiarity, we humans tend to persist in doing what we've always done in the way we've always done it. To

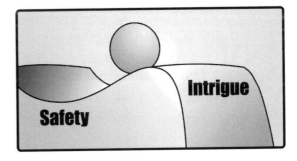

move people forward, we have to coax them out of their comfort nests to see what alternatives may be out there.

One powerful way to begin the process of change and to interest people in learning is to intrigue them. When we're truly fascinated by something mysterious, surprising, powerful, or inexplicable, we tend to push fears out of our minds while searching for explanations and understanding. This is a gateway to effective learning experiences.

As we explore connecting with learners' minds, both cognitively and affectively, we'll be looking at ways to intrigue learners and put them on the path to learning through three major approaches:

1. Personalization—Is this really about me?

LID Tip: Letting learners feel that the experience is all about them and their needs pulls learners in, captivating their attention and energy, at least for a while.

2. Humanization and dramatic impact—Isn't this going to be boring?

LID Tip: Emotional connection is critical to energizing the learner's full participation and attention.

3. Authenticity and situational fidelity—Is successful performance really like this?

LID Tip: A great context can stimulate learner imagination, set perceptions, and make events feel real, even through quite limited simulations.

E Is for Empower

Mr. Wizard knew it was important to let kids do at least some steps of his TV "experiments." As we watched (those of us old enough to remember will recall), we all wanted to get in there and participate. Mr. Wizard knew never to embarrass or humiliate. There was no risk. We innately know it's in the doing that we can really have fun (and learn). Intricacies that we overlook so easily while watching someone else perform a task can stop us dead in our tracks when we try to do the same task learned only through observation. Ever watch someone demonstrate how to use a new software product, then try it yourself? Did you realize you were far less prepared than you thought? To empower learners we have to give them some controls and let them do things—seemingly real things, not just advancing to the next slide or answering questions. From an LID perspective, this involves a two-way communication: presenting information and listening.

1. Visual clarity—Can I understand this?

LID Tip: Consistency and persistency of design elements put learners at ease, help them know what to expect, and permit focus on what's most important.

2. Input and control—Can I do it as I really would?

LID Tip: Input gestures and controls need to naturally translate the learner's intentions into actions, for example, allow direct manipulation of objects rather than using extra buttons and controls that have no real-world analogy.

O Is for Orchestrate

It's one thing to provide an open lab and let learners loose in it. But this can be fruitless, not to mention dangerous and expensive. Thinking again of the wildly successful *Watch Mr. Wizard*, star and scientist Don Herbert carefully orchestrated each situation so kids could see scientific principles at work while working with familiar objects. He would compare how things work in some situations (paper burns when it is surrounded by air) and when they

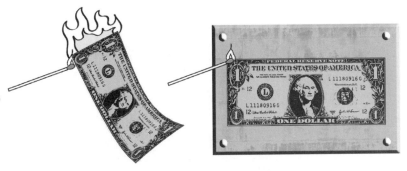

don't (paper money won't ignite when tightly pressed against metal). This took planning, design, development, and testing. Such are the requirements of LID. To successfully orchestrate learning events, we can:

1. Build on performance-based learning objectives—What can I do after completing this?

LID Tip: To achieve needed outcomes, it's important to contrive situations that reveal potential outcomes in obvious ways and inform learners of their progress.

2. Challenge and help—Will you help me when I need help?

LID Tip: Learners will continue to face challenges if they are rewarded by clear outcomes of their efforts, both successes and failures, and as long as help comes when it's needed (and not much sooner).

3. Provide performance-relevant controls—Is that how it works?

LID Tip: Provide a collection of learner controls appropriate to the learner's readiness to handle content complexity. Increase fidelity steadily toward real-life controls as learner skills advance.

The Language of Learning Event Design

In designing an interface, whether for a fruit juicer, an airplane cockpit, or an e-learning application, one must identify and become familiar with the components, functions, and controls. The components and controls of a juicer and an airplane cockpit seem evident on inspection, although perhaps not understandable without explanation of their functions, but what are the components, functions, and controls of e-learning? They're not so obvious.

Learner interface design components can seem innumerable, obscure, and indeterminate, as almost any type of interaction can be created in e-learning software. Screen layout can be varied in an infinite number of ways. Timing, animation, and media, in addition to the infinite functional and conditional variations achievable through programmed logic, allow every e-learning application to be unique in appearance and behavior. Are these myriad components what we're talking about when we learn to create effective learner interfaces?

Well, yes, these are the components of which interfaces are built. But we need a functional and more holistic way of identifying the interface components of e-learning applications to understand, compare, create, and use them effectively. Specifically, for learner interface design, we need to organize learner interface design concepts, approaches, and principles in a way that does not bury them in the mechanics of interface components, but rather sorts them by the roles they play in creating effective learning. In short, we need a language for discussing the critical details of learning events.

CCAF to the Rescue

As we discussed in *Designing Successful e-Learning*, the previous volume of this series, there is a unifying, foundational view of instructional events that is useful both for designing and describing instructional designs. It is useful for all instructional delivery means, but is perhaps of special value for both instructor-led and e-learning events. We're talking here about Context, Challenge, Activity, and Feedback—or simply "CCAF" in our designer jargon.

CCAF provides a new lens uniquely suited for viewing LID. It helps keep focus on the contribution that interface components can make, not just to usability, but more importantly to learning outcomes. In some occasions, looking at designs from the perspectives of context, challenge, activity, and feedback reveals that too much emphasis on ease of use and minimized cognitive burden actually conflicts with good

learner interface design and weakens the potential power of learning events. Really? Yes. It's hard to learn to really perform tasks if you don't practice performing them. Really.

The next chapter provides a refresher on the critical concepts of context, challenge, activity, and feedback in preparation for using CCAF as a learner interface design framework. It provides a way for communicating, discussing, and examining the many design decisions that define learning events. Following the next chapter, we'll return to a close examination of CEO—connect, empower, and orchestrate.

3 | CCAF

Yes, learning events can be complex things. Live instructors are often quite unaware of the amazing things they do when working with their students. Live instructors, especially the good ones, are constantly assessing changing situations, experimenting, and making adjustments. The awesome complexity of what they do when they teach successfully becomes particularly apparent when we try to replicate such learning events in today's technology without real-time pairing of teachers and students.

Even if our technology could be as alert, aware, and perceptive as good instructors are, noting when some students are engaged and keeping quiet so as not to inhibit their progress, finding ways to inspire and refocus those students who aren't coping, providing examples relating to noted interests of individual students, providing a push, a challenge, a consolation, or a summary at just the right time—even if it could do all this, the design, development, and programming would be tasks far outside usual budgetary limitations.

Of course, computers aren't people. Attempts to replicate learning events in e-learning that would be effective under the leadership of

a talented instructor fail miserably. To succeed, many elements must be deleted or adapted to work in e-learning, and some portions may adapt well. So how does one know what will and will not work?

Describing Learning Events

Whether moving content from one medium to another or creating new courses of instruction, it's been difficult to talk about, define, compare, and contrast learning events. Sure, we can talk about content. We can define instructional objectives. We can write scripts and storyboard.

And with all of this, it has remained difficult to effectively communicate the architecture of an instructional event at a usefully descriptive level of detail. Not until, that is, we realized that learning events, regardless of delivery medium, can be described effectively using the framework of context, challenge, activity, and feedback—CCAF.

Context

It's hard to imagine a good learning event that isn't built on a solid, content-related context, while, conversely, there are many examples of regrettable e-learning in which designers failed to provide any context at all or used a regrettable one. Context is the foundation—the

critical base for successful learning experiences.

The context can answer such important questions as:

➤ When would I do this?
➤ Where would I do this?
➤ Why would I do this?
➤ What would I use to do this?
➤ What would I need to know to do this?

Note that building on a context naturally puts emphasis on things the learner is learning to do. Knowledge acquisition is immediately put in its proper place as an enabler to the goal of successful performance.

Poor Context

Lack of a context makes learning harder and retention shorter. Learning is harder because each piece of information is an isolated nugget unless the learner can think of some way to associate it with others. It can be like learning lists of trivia. Retention is shorter because there are no associations to reinforce and stimulate memory.

In today's enthusiasm for "rapid" authoring, especially template-based rapid authoring, much e-learning is being built using either no discernable context or unfortunate and irrelevant contexts. We receive no content-specific context from bullet-point slides, for example. Presentations of information listed in little bites followed by multiple-choice questions generally convey little or no context. Slides and bullet points, even if painstakingly indented, don't engagingly and emotionally convey the seriousness of a terminally ill cancer patient, the worry of a challenging sales pitch from a competitor, or the outrage of a manager poorly addressing a sexual harassment accusation. While it's possible to add some context into a multiple-choice question stem, *When a customer returns a product purchased from one of our competitors*, such quickly framed contexts tend to perform too much of the task the learner should perform, such as assessing the situation from visual or auditory cues, or provide too little detail to make the situation and the learner's response realistic.

Quiz game contexts, such as *Jeopardy* and *Wheel of Fortune*, offer content-neutral contexts. Such games are intentionally designed to be neutral with respect to content so that a broad array of information can be used equally well to gener-

ate games. Using content-neutral contexts is perhaps an expedient, but unfortunate and misguided, approach to creating learning events. One might meet budget and time constraints, minimize needs for creativity and subject-matter expertise, but ultimately fritter away the money and time invested and also the opportunity to build something of lasting value.

Perhaps even worse is a particular content-neutral "context" I've seen created with shocking frequency: the depiction of a classroom. On the screen, a blackboard is shown from the perspective of a student seated among other students at individual desks. A teacher is pointing to the blackboard or screen on which slides are presented. You, as a learner, can

and limitations and, because of the restrictions of technology, degrade the experience even further?

Good Context

Good contexts make learning interactions meaningful by relating content to actual performance situations—facing travelers at a ticket counter, discussing cable service options with a customer over the phone, flying a plane in stormy weather, confronting a disorganized stockroom, starting a new job. Even these brief descriptive phrases create mental pictures that resonate with learners and start them thinking of tasks they might need to perform well.

Good contexts make subtle things subtle, as they would be in real life, not unrealistically obvious. They place things where they would be placed, reflect consequences of actions in a realistic manner, provide the behavioral options that would typically be available, and so on. To the extent that contexts are not arbitrarily restrictive (either through design or because of technology limitations) and represent the salient aspects of typical performance situations, we call them *authentic contexts*. The greater the authenticity,

click the screen to advance slides, click images of students to see questions they might ask or how they would answer a question from the teacher, click on the teacher for clarification or an example, click on a dictionary to look up words, and so on. I've seen many people beam with pride after creating yet another instance of such an e-learning application—most with fewer interactive capabilities than these.

Look, you can even click on the door to take a break! The instructor will announce, "It's time for recess!"

In e-learning, we try to overcome some of the weaknesses and limitations of typical classroom learning. Why would someone want to re-create the trappings of a classroom with all its faults, implications, the easier it will be for learners to transfer their learning to actual real-life performance. A primary requirement of learner interface design is to make contexts as authentic as possible.

A good context piques learner curiosity, generates questions, and answers them—such questions as those listed above: *What might I be doing? When would I do this? Where would I do this? Why would I do this? What would I use to do this? What would I need to know to do this?*

A good context provides the basis for the other three CCAF components. It lends purpose and meaningfulness to challenges. It provides an arena or stage for activities. And it allows feedback to be expressed in terms of results or consequences of actions taken.

Challenge

Quite some years ago, in conversation with Seymour Papert, a proponent and researcher of discovery learning, he relayed an anecdote that I now see as instructive about the importance of context: A teenage boy was having trouble with multi-column subtraction. Asked, *What is 500 minus 50?*, the boy responded, *150.* Professor Papert then asked him, *So if you bought a some gum for 50 cents, gave the clerk a five-dollar bill, and got $1.50 back, it would be fair?* The boy responded instantly, *You think I'm a fool, man? I'd get my whole $4.50 back or we'd have trouble.*

Not everyone liked math "story problems" when I was in grade school (although I actually did), but there can be an undeniable value in them. Challenges take on relevance when they build on a context. Context helps learners visualize situations and how they would respond, all of which enhances focus, depth of learning, retention, and transfer to real-world situations. But what constitutes good and bad challenges? What are the learner interface components that make them effective?

Poor Challenges

Just having a challenge doesn't mean a learning event is well designed. There are many ways, unfortunately, to make challenges ineffective. Here are some of them:

➢ No Context

We've noted already that one way to create poor learning challenges is to make them devoid of context. We've all seen many context-less challenges in school.

What's 500 minus 50? Name three elements of . . . Scuba diving is an _____-_____ sport ("equipment-intensive", of course—a real question in a diving certification exam!).

➢ Irrelevant

Another popular way to make challenges ineffective is to make them irrelevant. *If a train leaves Clarion at 10 a.m. traveling at 50 miles per hour, heading toward Minneapolis, 180 miles away, and another train leaves Minneapolis at the same time, traveling toward Clarion at 60 miles per hour, at what time will they meet?* Someone is undoubtedly interested in this. Name a seventh grader who is.

Although there are contexts that make this algebraic challenge understandable, most students who face these kinds of challenges in school can't *imagine* (and that's

a key word) actually needing to solve such a problem. Who cares? If the challenge and context are not working together to make it crystal clear why the learner should care—why the learner should acquire the skills necessary to meet the challenge—then you have a poor challenge. What most people retain from these classic academic challenges is that they found them frustrating, hate them, and can't remember how to solve them. Quite the opposite of the intended outcome: recognizing that algebra is a great problem-solving tool and being able to use it whenever needed.

➢ Embarrassing

Challenges pose some risk to learners. *Will I look stupid? I suppose everyone else gets this.* A major advantage of e-learning is that

it can provide a private learning environment in which learners can take risks and have no fear of public embarrassment. Challenges shouldn't panic learners.

I never get these right; they're so frustrating. I don't know why I get these problems; the answers are obvious. Challenges that are too difficult or beneath the skill level of learners have obvious negative consequences. Yet another advantage of e-learning is that it can match levels of challenge to each learner's readiness and change the level as the learner's skill progresses.

➢ Obscure

Poor challenges arise when poor user interface designs make it difficult for learners to understand and use whatever options and choices they are given. Combating poor interface mechanics; not being able to understand directions, the situation, or the problem; and not receiving needed help and feedback are all common design faults. They create challenges, sure enough. These decidedly poor challenges interfere with, rather than enhance, the learning experience.

Good Challenges

We love the energy people exhibit when they're playing games and wish we saw that same exuberance and intensive learning when they were interacting with our e-learning. What's fueling game players, keeping them focused, motivated, and intent on doing better? Challenge.

What doesn't most e-learning have? Good challenges.

Challenge and risk go hand in hand. When are we most alert, scanning for options, evaluating each possible action we might take? When we're at risk. When are we not paying attention, trying to stay focused (if not just awake), wondering when we can do something else? When we're bored.

Challenge is a major antidote to boredom and therefore a treasured tool of learning event designers. Characteristics of good challenges are, of course, opposite to the characteristics of poor challenges listed above. Good challenges:

> Build on context

> Are relevant to the learner in a way the learner understands

> Cause learners to visualize and anticipate successful real-world performance

> Are safe and pose no risk of humiliation or embarrassment

> Don't panic learners

> Are neither too hard nor too easy for the individual learner

> Arise out of the skills to be learned, rather than from complications, ambiguities, or other weaknesses in the interface design

Activity

Two types of critical activity need to be rehearsed in order to build skills and readiness to perform: mental and physical. Because we can't readily observe mental activity, we use physical activity to reflect mental behavior. Typing *aardvark* or speaking the letters in order out loud are

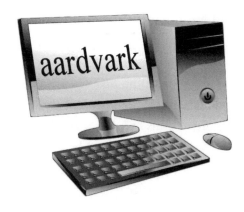

physical activities we can assess. We assume they were preceded by mental activity that recalled the proper spelling, which was then translated into finger or vocal movement.

e-Learning is restrictive in the type of physical activities we can observe through its hardware and software. While amazing progress is being made in the ability to directly assess brain activity and determine what people are thinking, we are typically restricted to relatively simple mouse and keyboard gestures. At times we have had primitive touch and/or stylus input, as with the PLATO project, for example, and we are now (finally) seeing touch input capabilities becoming more common and adept. Voice recognition is also finding its footing and will continue to become more widely available. Video recognition

is a latecomer, but is perhaps gaining ground faster than any other sensory technology.

Still, most of today's e-learning situations have very little perceptive awareness. Our systems don't know whether the learner is even present, let alone whether the learner is focused and engaged or perhaps watching an overlaid YouTube window. We therefore need to take full advantage of the precious few interface capabilities we have.

Poor Activity

There are three types of poor learning activities:

1. Those that have no resemblance to the physical performance needed and thus do not provide performance practice
2. Those that fail to engage the same cognitive behavior as real-life performance will require and thus do not lead to necessary mental abilities to perform
3. Those that poorly reflect cognitive activity so that we cannot tell whether learners are making progress toward performance readiness

Perhaps because of the limited gestures today's computers recognize, or perhaps because of the tradition of measuring learning outcomes poorly and inappropriately, it's tempting to use inappropriate activities for both learning and assessment events.

When your trainees deliver the outstanding customer service you are teaching them to provide, will they provide it by checking off answers to multiple-choice questions? Probably

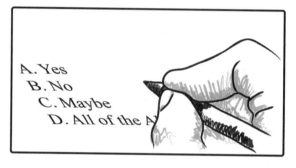

not. When your managers provide excellent leadership, will they do it through drag-and-drop mouse gestures? Probably not. These are mismatched physical activities.

If you can answer questions about how to do something, does this mean you can do it? Of course not. The target [I feel silly writing this obvious fact] is not developing the skill to answer questions, it's developing the skill to perform. Yet many educational and training programs are focused on standard-form post-test questions as a measure of suc-

cess. These are mismatched learning and measurement activities.

Truly, if answering questions is the success you need, then you should be teaching people to answer questions. Both the physical and cognitive skills being rehearsed will be directly transferable. But if answering standard-form questions isn't the success you need, the activities your e-learning provides must resemble the targeted outcome behaviors as closely as possible.

This is also true for the cognitive behaviors you want to develop. Multiple-choice questions sometimes provide a structure resembling counterparts that exist in the real world, but often only create overly simplified exercises. In asking you to select from alternative answers, multiple-choice questions identify the alternatives to consider— and usually a small number of alternatives at that. Would those alternatives be apparent in actual performance conditions? Would identifying alternatives be part of successful performance (an activity denied by the multiple-choice question itself)? Would the learner see possible actions as related to the challenge at hand? *(B) Use the pillow as a fire extinguisher.*

Although, structurally, clicking objects in a room is very similar to clicking answers to a multiple-choice question, the activity is a very different cognitive exercise.

In the exercise shown below, learners are asked to click on each safety hazard and follow the instructions to choose the appropriate warning signal and then select the best way(s) to handle that safety hazard. How many safety hazards can you identify?

Good Activity
Physical Activity

Some e-learning activities, like creating a spreadsheet, using call-center software, creating a budget, filling out an insurance claim form, or completing a timesheet, can replicate performance skills being taught with full fidelity. Requiring the learners to do exactly what they would do when using actual software applications makes for a good learning activity.

Other e-learning activities can be quite similar to their real-world

Screen capture courtesy of Essilor of America, Inc.

counterparts, if not identical. Testing voltages at specific points on an electronics card, setting a navigation system's destination, using a calculator, setting the controls on a lens-grinding machine. These activities can achieve a sufficient level of fidelity or authenticity in the physical motion component and require full authenticity of the learner's cognitive activity.

Cognitive Activity

"Don't make me think" is an appropriate mantra of user interface designers. In general, we want interfaces of tools to be so natural or transparent that users don't have to think about them much at all to use them. What users expect to have happen in response to input gestures is what actually happens.

In contrast, e-learning is all about thinking. We'd prefer the banner, "Make me think!" Thinking needs to be rehearsed,

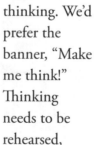

just as physical activities need to be practiced, for skills to be developed and retained.

Sometimes the performance of a

skill, such as playing tennis or the cello, requires unique motor skills, but sometimes the preponderance of a skill is cognitive. Prior learning also factors into the modality of a learning task. Once one is able to read and write, for example, it's not necessary to learn new motor skills to add or subtract numbers. For practicing various mathematic skills, it doesn't really matter whether the results are written with pencil and paper or are entered via keyboard. In these cases, e-learning is well-suited to support all of the necessary activity.

Some have concluded that soft skills, such as leadership, customer support, and medical patient interviewing, cannot be taught well by computer because the computer is ill-equipped to assess performance of such skills. It's true that there are physical activity components that are difficult if not impossible to assess electronically, but there are often major cognitive components, prerequisite to successful physical performance, that can be taught well with e-learning. Years ago, the IRS offered training that played video segments of angry and/or upset taxpayers. Agents were taught techniques of responding to various emotional outbursts and were much better prepared for volatile encounters when they actually happened.

Somewhat similarly, work at Carnegie Mellon University put learners into ethical dilemmas dealing with such difficult situations as suffering, terminally ill patients petitioning the court to permit their euthanasia or suicide. Learners were to decide what should happen, balancing ethics and the law in the process. The opportunity to study multiple cases portrayed dramatically in part by actual patients and their families, and to take time to adjust to the gravity and vicissitude of such situations, allowed for and supported essential cognitive activity for properly handling them.

The physical activity in the IRS case was important, as not only what was said to enraged taxpayers, but also how it was said, was critical.

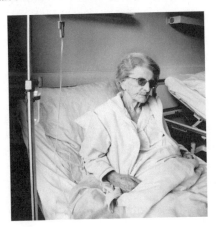

Learners could witness the approach they selected by playing the appropriate video. They could see how proper intonation was critical to success. This feedback undoubtedly shaped their own performance. But to achieve the full set of necessary skills, practice of the physical skills was critical. Nevertheless, e-learning provided a large part of the necessary training.

Augmented Reality

Of course, e-learning need not stand entirely on its own and is always best with supporting external activities. Activities that cannot be replicated in whole through e-learning and those that cannot be evaluated by e-learning can still be part of the solution. e-Learning can do what it does best; then observers can input results of external activities, such as practice and evaluation sessions, so that e-learning can accumulate performance information and provide remediation when deemed appropriate.

The big message here: Good learning activity stimulates and rehearses to the fullest extent possible the physical and cognitive activity that is needed for good real-world performance.

Feedback

Even with a great context supporting effective challenges and activities, e-learning can and does fail without good feedback. Without feedback, learners might well be practicing ineffective skills and drawing faulty conclusions without knowing it. The means of providing good feedback aren't as obvious as one might expect.

Poor Feedback

That's correct. Great job, Johnny. Johnny probably liked this feedback, but it wasn't good feedback. It's nice to have some individual recognition, but not even much personalization of feedback comes from simply inserting the learner's name. *Why was the response correct? Why was it*

"great"? Was it really or are you just pleased I finally got an answer correct?

That's wrong. Try again. This classic feedback is easy to write and program. It can be used for all wrong answers. Talk about rapid authoring! But it's terrible. *Apparently, I should just keep guessing. In fact, I should probably always just guess quickly and see if I got it.* No thinking necessary here.

No, Sarah. The first step is to review the job functions that each newly hired person will be required to perform. Although we generally think immediate, corrective feedback is the best feedback, such feedback may trump the opportunity for learners to evaluate their own performance. Poor feedback like this actually interrupts the process of learning. Expert performers know when their performance is good (and otherwise). So this ability—enabling learners to assess the quality of their performance—is actually part of our targeted outcomes.

Good. You've picked up the pliers. Now what part of the engine will you adjust with them? This sounds like we have a challenge to be solved in multiple steps. Good. It feels like an authentic challenge. But the feedback is preventing what might otherwise be a terrific learning event. *I don't really know how to do this, so I just clicked a tool to see whether it's the right one. If it is, the feedback will tell me. I can then eliminate some of the things I might try doing because I wouldn't use pliers for them.* Feedback can have powerful effects on learners, both positive and negative. It directs cognitive activity as well as physical. In this case, the feedback sets up an unintended game. The learner starts trying to find the correct answer through efficient elimination of e-learning presented alternatives, using feedback as a crutch and response strategy in lieu of thinking about what could be causing the engine's faulty performance. The feedback is actually taking the learner's focus away from the problem to be addressed. What learners might well carry away with them is not how to fix engines, but rather a strategy: *Always choose the wrench first, because if feedback tells you it's the wrong tool, there are then only three mechanical adjustments left that could be causing the engine problem.*

Good Feedback

Good feedback should:

➢ Cause learners to think
➢ Very clearly present the consequences of actions taken
➢ Teach evaluation criteria so learners can evaluate their own performance
➢ Recognize the individual as an individual and communicate quite precisely how he or she is doing

Juan, your decision to give the gerbil fewer sunflower seeds was a good correction. See what he's doing now? The gerbil is eating other nutrients he needs to be healthy. Excellent.

Where possible, it's often best to use visual media to demonstrate the consequences of learner activities. Additional commentary may be helpful, especially if the learner is new to the subject or seems to be floundering.

Sometimes the best feedback is another challenge. *Sarah, why do you think your interviews with job applicants didn't give you the information you need?* This feedback may cause Sarah to review the process decisions she made and realize she forgot to base her questions on identified job functions. Instead of pointing out her mistake directly, help her think through the situation. Good feedback helps people focus, think, and practice.

It's certainly fine to use the learner's name, but a much more meaningful form of personalization is to reflect in the feedback what the learner did, comment on any change (improvement or degradation from previous responses), and then stress the consequences. Effective feedback for novices is different from the feedback that works best for more advanced learners. Novices may just need to explore, to try any response to the challenge they can think of and see what happens.

Part Two

Learner Interface
Design Guidelines

4 | C Is for Connect

Welcome, students, to Chemistry 101. A few notes before we get started.

First, I've taught this class here at Wilbur College for fourteen years now. This is a difficult class, and we know at least a third of you won't make it. So let me advise you in the strongest terms possible: study hard, keep up, and get help if you need it.

Second, the rules. I wouldn't be able to teach this course year after year without rules. Don't ask for exceptions. Don't bother me with excuses. Late papers, for example, will not be scored. You will receive no credit for them. The complete set of rules is printed out for your reference. Take a set from the stacks at the back of the room when you leave today. There's one copy per person. I do not have extras.

Once again, welcome to Chemistry 101. I hope you'll get a lot out of it. It's an important course. Your eligibility to stay in the program depends on your doing well in it. No questions? OK, let's get started.

Attention. Attention! ATTENTION!!

If I don't have your attention, it doesn't matter what's written here, does it? If your learners are not attending to the events around them, they might as well be somewhere else.

It's a simple fact. Attention is necessary for learning. We have to connect with learners, and learners need to pay attention to content to learn. And the connection needs to be

Яapid readeR

- Connecting with learners starts with getting their attention and interest.

- If we don't show interest in our learners, they will remain detached and superficial participants.

- Reflect your knowledge of your learners by designing a program that is fun, rewarding, and appropriate for them.

an effective one—one that not only focuses attention but also energizes, enthuses, resonates, fascinates, and entices.

Fear can certainly motivate learning (*At least a third of you won't make it*), but fear also exhausts learners and tends to focus learners on the wrong things. Instead of imagining the great accomplishments one might have with newly acquired skills, fearful learners tend to concentrate on what will happen to them if they do poorly. Fear ultimately makes learning harder.

The most powerful learning experiences, described in our terms, are those in which a presented context focuses learner attention. Challenges appear to energize thinking. Options to act allow learners to apply and test their reasoning. Feedback, presented largely as consequences to actions, helps learners evaluate their own behavior. Guidance and explanations pop up in response to the learner's request for them and automatically when the learner seems to need it, but volumes of information are not thrust on learners at every possible moment, interrupting the opportunities for learners to evaluate, synthesize, and construct relationships for themselves.

Attention Versus Distraction

If learners are not connecting rationally and emotionally with the context, challenge, activities, and feedback (CCAF)—if they're off in another space or just simply not ready for the level of instructional content—they will metabolize little of what the experience could otherwise offer.

The whole process begins with connection. It's the first door that learners must pass through. Perhaps the most important tests of LID are whether it (1) succeeds at initially gaining learner attention and then (2) sustains involvement. Just as when we read an engaging book, we are learning, feeling, seeing with our whole minds. The attention we need in e-learning is similar. It isn't just eyes on the screen or inserted earphones playing event sounds and narrations—a dalliance with the computer. Focus must be on germane components and events so that learners can then begin to sympathize, empathize, visualize, and experience—and through interactivity become part of the experience themselves.

Spinning logos, twinkling buttons, and jazzy background music

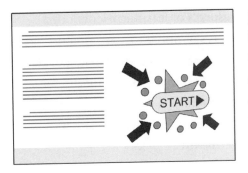

can attract attention. Too much attention. Lengthy introductions and orientations, too many navigational controls, and even too much feedback siphon off engagement from the experience as well. These LID faux pas can and often do diminish the attention we need for learning events to have impact. We have to think as would a director of a play. Where do we want the audience looking? What do we want the audience feeling? What do we want the audience thinking?

Functional Connection

Learning experiences form a functional connection with learners that the mere presentation of information cannot do. When learners have given us their initial attention, they typically do so conditionally. Whether it was novelty that snagged their gaze, mystery that conjured speculation, or the promise of something of value in return for their participation, learners just inside the front menu hang close to the door unless a second level of engagement develops to warrant continued presence. This is when it's quite critical to deepen the functional connection.

Presenting a lengthy orientation, thrusting out lists of terms and bullet points, or dishing out volumes of information, while very common indeed, are simply dysfunctional approaches. Learners swivel on their heels and mentally, if not physically, race toward the exit. Attention lost. Connection lost.

To prevent sabotaging a nascent connection, we designers need to focus on the learner's probable state of mind. Learners need to stop questioning whether they want to continue—whether venturing forward will be a reasonable use of their time—and lose themselves in the learning experience with full participation. Reasonable questions—*Is this about me? Is this appropriate for me? Is this going to be boring? Is it going to take too much effort? Do I really want to do what this is teaching me? Will I be able to?*—should cease to become barriers either because satisfactory answers are apparent or because the attraction of the experience dissipates the angst.

aspects of learning events? Three ways of doing this are establishing:

1. Relevance and personalization
2. Humanization and dramatic impact
3. Authenticity and situational fidelity

These are established, of course, through carefully devised contexts and the other CCAF components (challenge, activity, and feedback).

Of the four CCAF components, context typically takes the stage first. If it's well designed, the context addresses some questions learners are likely to have. *What's it all about? What's this going to be like? What will I have to do? Is this going to be hard? How long will it take?*

Initial attention is likely to be fairly high driven by these entry questions, perhaps a little anxiety of the unknowns and simply shifting into a different activity. Context therefore represents the designer's initial opportunity to focus and heighten productive attention. Ideally, the context will hit learners with a combination of stimuli that simultaneously and instantly start learners thinking while provoking their emotions. Further challenging the designer, I might add, we'd

As soon as possible, learners need to move into contextual situations that cause them to suspend their disbelief. They need to feel they are actually on a sales call, actually tracking down an electrical fault, actually responsible for selecting or rejecting proposed products, or actually handling a customer call.

They need to feel an opportunity for success and at least a little risk of failure. Whatever the skills to be learned, the context and challenge need to create a believable situation that connects with the learner and begins the individual's learning experience.

So how do we avoid distractions and connect learners to the salient like to see this accomplished with a minimum of words—especially on-screen words.

Let's review three powerful ways of connecting with learners.

Relevance and Personalization

There are trivial and superficial ways to personalize learning experiences, such as inserting a person's name in text. *That was the correct answer, John.* While people usually like to have their names used in conversation, this use of names is barely more significant than having your name appear on junk mail advertising. It gets noticed, but it seems manipulative and annoying. It's a stretch to call this personalization.

Making instruction relevant to the individual, however, by adapting as much to individual needs and interests as possible—that's personalization that matters. It matters because it helps connect with learners, makes them realize that because they are who they are, the learning events will be uniquely theirs. We're not going to waste their time, but rather maximize the use of it.

Much training is offered with obscured relevance to trainees, if indeed relevance was really much of a consideration. The same is true about academic courses.

Trust me. Someday you'll be glad you know this. Really? When will that be? After I've forgotten it all?

You'll never have to do this in the field, but it's important for you to know how it works. Why? Couldn't I just practice the tasks I will actually do?

Communicating high-tech information to foreigners is illegal. We'll cover ways to protect our company's restricted information. I'm the receptionist and don't have access to any restricted information. I really have other things I need to do today.

This sexual harassment training is extremely important. I've never had a problem in all the years I've been a manager. Besides, I'm sure I can handle any situation that comes up. We're just talking about mutual respect here.

Just saying something is important doesn't convince learners that it actually is. In each of the actual cases above, the content was, in fact, relevant to learners assigned to it. The relevance just wasn't apparent to learners at the beginning when it would have been easiest to establish and use it to connect with learners. Learner interest and motivation dropped immediately upon joining into these courses due to the way they were designed, and for many it never returned.

Is This About Me?

Relevance is very helpful for reaching instructional goals. Understood relevance can boost energy and involvement. Such a boost can be invaluable, especially when a course of instruction is mandated and learners are therefore a bit adverse to the whole thing. *This is an important course. Your eligibility to stay in the program depends on your doing well in it.* One of the reasons performance support and just-in-time learning have appeal is that they're seen as relevant—being offered when application is immediate and useful. Learners appreciate the help they offer.

It seems almost too obvious to mention, but learners need to see the relevance of what they are learning to have sustained enthusiasm for it. It also helps a great deal when learners realize that the program adjusts as they succeed or struggle and as they express specific interests and desires.

When It's About the Content

Of course, sometimes curiosity is the driver, and personal goals are fluid. In general, browsing learners are looking to make connections on their own. *Should I consider a reverse mortgage? How is taffy made? How can I prevent this thing from rusting? What is a widget?*

When the goal is exposure to content, when it absolutely and truly is just exposure and not skill development, one can actually argue that challenges, so crucial for energizing most learning events, may not be necessary. Challenges are especially valuable when a performance skill is targeted. Through graduated challenges, we can keep learners engaged and working at successively more valuable levels. Challenges can just be fun in and of themselves, not necessarily leading anywhere. But when learners are only seeking information or when organizations simply want to generously offer information for any purposes people might have, then challenges become optional. Relevance and personalization remain important, however, if we hope learners won't quickly abandon us. A whimsical, humorous, artistic, surprising, or other theatrical genre can make the browsing experience rewarding enough to sustain learner interest. In this case, the way to personalize the experience is to give learners maximum control.

In the exercise shown, fascinating information about the rich history of a banking enterprise, its evolution, and creation are delivered so interactively that it is difficult not to browse through every morsel of contained information.

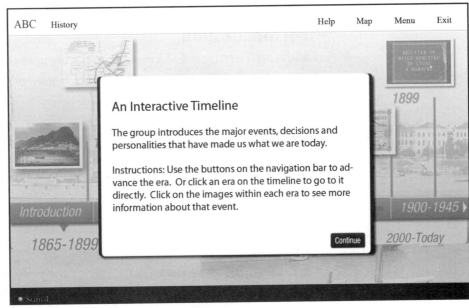

Introductory screen

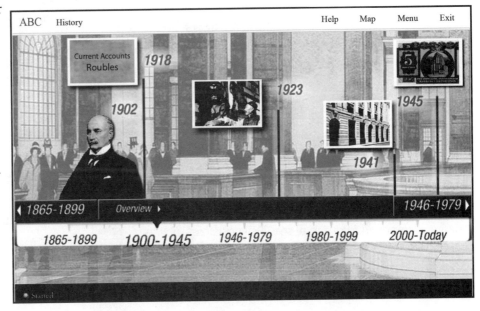

Each section of the timeline displays the featured events and accomplishments of that selected time frame. The learner can easily scroll through decades of information.

Relevance and Personalization
Viewed Through CCAF

How then do we connect with learners? Analyzing the process of connecting with learners through the CCAF lens, we can see the following guidelines for creating relevance and personalizing the e-learning experience:

Context

C1. Demonstrate that you know your learners.

C1-a). Meeting of minds. Create a context that matches the probable mindset of the audience. Do you have learners who are comfortable with reading? Are they used to solving problems on their own or as members of a team? Do they expect to see tools, machines, or instruments?

C1-b). Hero for a day. Present a situation in which each learner can easily visualize himself or herself having and managing an important responsibility—a situation that can lead to a proud success.

C1-c). Please identify yourself. If you are teaching the same content to learners who have varying skills, are on different career paths, or are likely to have different definable interests in the content and skills to be learned, provide choices or ask a couple of questions to select a context that can be meaningful to the individual.

How to best use the design guidelines:

In this and following chapters, practical ideas and guidelines are identified for each of the CEO principles. Guidelines are labeled for reference in the examples found in Chapter 9. A downloadable reference guide of all the guidelines is available through the Allen Interactions Web site, http://info.alleninteractions.com/e-learning-interface-reference-guide.

Challenge

C2. Select meaningful and beneficial challenges.

C2-a). Why should they care? If the role you're asking the learners to play isn't the same as the role you're asking them to play for learning, explain why it's helpful to assume the responsibilities of this role now.

C2-b). Make challenges challenging. Challenges should be neither too simple nor too difficult. Most importantly, they should require each individual to think. If prior assessment is not available to calibrate the appropriate level of challenge, try a moderate challenge at first, provide extensive help for those who happen to need it, and set the next challenge either higher or lower depending on the amount of help that was required.

Activity

C3. Activities should relate to what learners do now and will do after skill development.

C3-a). Match performance modalities. Repair technicians probably like to fix things; they like puzzles and problem solving and are visual. Don't have them write essays. Creative people hope to find that multiple solutions exist, or at least that there are multiple valid paths for arriving at solutions. Make sure they can explore options.

C3-b). True tasks. The activity should involve tasks that learners could and would actually carry out in the real world. As learners near proficiency, available support mechanisms should be reduced (or expanded) to represent those that will actually be available.

Feedback

C4. It's not just what you say, but how you say it.

C4-a). Stay in character. To personalize the experience, the feedback should be expressed in a form most meaningful and directly related to the learner. For example, rather than just showing that profits of the company dropped because of a lost sale, the company in the event story might announce layoffs as a result of poor business performance and the learner, most regrettably, is being let go. That's getting personal, huh?

Humanization and Dramatic Impact

Even before learners start to wonder whether the experience is going to be boring, you can hit them between the brain hemispheres, alerting both the logical and emotive person that something interesting is about to commence. Start telling a story. Build human interest. Create a mystery. Do something humorous. Do something that lets learners know you care about their experience and about them. We want

people employing their emotional intelligence as well as their cognitive intelligence, and to do that, we need to stimulate both intelligences.

Content-centric designers agonize over organizing, structuring, and presenting content. The more perfectly content is presented, it's reasoned, the stronger the message is to learners. Unfortunately, it's not a good message that gets through. What comes through is the message that this is all about content and that you, "the learner," are the, um, fortunate recipient.

Learner-centric designers orchestrate learning events around the learners and the experience they will have. These designers consider such things as, *How can the experience be rewarding? How can it be fun? How can it be adaptive? What controls can we give learners?* Asking these questions is a good way to begin thinking about dramatic impact. It's a good way to be sure your learners will experience learning that is not about content, but rather about them, their benefit, and their success.

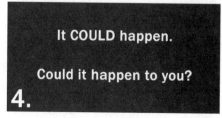

Humanization and Dramatic Impact
Viewed Through CCAF

Learning experiences that connect on a human level and have dramatic impact are built from context, challenge, activity, and feedback. These components come together most dramatically and impactfully when composed and joined together by someone who personally feels and enjoys the energy and power that come from the very knowledge and skills that the learners are acquiring. These are the inspiring people who can take household items, as did Mr. Wizard, and create experiences that have impact over a full lifetime. As much as possible, designers need to surround themselves with such people and attempt to become one themselves.

Here are some ways that successful designers use the basic components to humanize learning experiences and harness the power of dramatic impact:

Context
C5. Use theatrical devices.

C5-a). *It was a dark and stormy night,* but the project had to be finished on time. Janice was at her wit's end without hope until you *showed up.* Begin a story with someone or something at risk. Put the learner in a position to help. The risk might be the possibility of not achieving an important goal or losing an opportunity, job, or something of value. Use names and create characters of interest and energize emotion. Let a storyline provide a basis for sequencing learning activities.

C5-b). **Use conflict.** To personalize the experience, the feedback should be expressed in a form most meaningful for and directly related to the learner. Instead, for example, of just showing that profits of the company dropped because of a lost sale, the company in the event story might announce layoffs as a result of poor business performance and the learner, most regrettably, is being let go.

C5-c). Be funny. Laughing releases endorphins that make us feel good and want more. Incorporating humor doesn't mean you aren't also serious about providing an effective use of learner time. Learners appreciate efforts to "entertrain" or "edutain" them and will respond with their attention and participation, especially if your efforts are truly entertaining as well as beneficial.

C5-d). Just (let them) do it. Avoid lengthy instruction about how to work the e-learning application. The user interface and the learner interface should be sufficiently intuitive that people can figure most of it out as they go. Tool tips and gradually revealed controls can help here. We want the context to be a content-related situation, and we do not want learners delayed getting to it. Nor do we want their focus constantly yanked away to deal with navigation or other mechanics outside the context of the experience.

Challenge

C6. Nest dramatic human consequences in the challenge.

C6-a). Solve our problem— everyone's depending on you. Challenge, activity, and feedback must all build on context to provide the best learning experience. Dramatic challenges are those with outcomes that matter. They're rarely single-step, isolated tasks. They're often provoking and complicated. Answering an academic question doesn't make the grade (sorry). But performing a procedure to meet a customer's expectations, using a software application to accomplish a task critical to a project's success, and taking proper precautions at a crime scene to protect people nearby—these can be dramatic challenges that energize learning like nothing else can.

Activity

C7. Keep the story going.

C7-a). Think real, not academic. We often break complicated tasks down into tiny steps so that learners won't be overwhelmed with a challenge that's too great for them. This is a good thing to do, but it's often done such that learners lose the sense of the context and begin performing tasks that have only artificial, abstracted, or academic consequences. We want to keep everything as authentic as possible, so even if activities have to be simplified, try to keep them within the context of the story, process, or system. Instead of having learners perform tasks they aren't yet ready to do, have learners put preceding and/or following tasks in order and click to have them performed by others so that the excitement of actually performing part of a real task is achieved.

C7-b). Face up. Inclusion of photos of people humanizes the learning space. If part of a process is performed by someone, submitted to someone, or created for someone's benefit, let's interact with faces. Ask learners to move teams together, drag a photo of a person into position to perform a task, and otherwise work with "people" rather than just letting photos of people adorn the screen (which is better than not having photos at all).

Feedback

C8. The story continues.

C8-a). Prefer consequences to judgments. Consequences that build on each other have much more dramatic impact than isolated events. Judgment tends to terminate an escalating event or chop it into segments, so be reluctant to offer judgment. Rather, demonstrate the consequences of the learner's actions continuously as the learner works to meet challenges.

C8-b). Use media to make outcomes memorable. Video from a delighted or uncontrollably angry customer will be remembered. How about audio of a caller ranting about a recently serviced car having broken down in a very remote location? Late at night! In a storm! How about a scrapbook page of a peer-aged student winning first place in a science contest with smiling teachers and parents, a tall trophy, and an ecstatic kid?

Authenticity and Situational Fidelity

Some years ago when working on an expert system to diagnose medical diseases using artificial intelligence, we discovered that teaching physicians did not present in their

classrooms what they actually did in practice. When we confronted them with this fact, the doctors admitted that they didn't really know how they did what they did anymore, so they constructed a logical curriculum much like they learned from, thinking that if it worked for them, it should work for their students also.

Students in these programs soon recognize that what they're learning in the classroom is useful on exams and gets them through required courses, but they still have much practical knowledge to acquire. The practical knowledge is often more germane to their success as practicing physicians and is retained long after their "book learning" is forgotten. Making rounds with their teaching physician was critical to acquiring important skills, but even this left many gaps for students to fill for themselves.

To fully connect with learners and help them transfer new skills to post-learning performance, it's extremely helpful to create a context, a set of challenges, and activities that represent real situations, real challenges, and the actual behavioral solutions that will work. This is situational fidelity or authenticity.

Low-tech solutions. It's not necessary to spend wildly to create a sufficient illusion of authenticity. Yet careful thought must go into what is and is not necessary to achieve enough fidelity in the learning situation to evoke serious consideration on the part of the learner and to allow learners the opportunity to perform enough of the critical aspects of tasks that they won't be confounded by differences presented by real-world situations. This is all accomplished through careful construction of (you guessed it) context, challenge, activity, and feedback. Let's review some tips on how to do it.

Authenticity and Situational Fidelity
Viewed Through CCAF

Context
C9. Context is almost everything. Choose wisely.

C9-a). It's OK to exaggerate some learning contexts for dramatic or humorous impact, but as people move closer to completing a course of learning, it's very important that the context be as authentic as possible. That is, the situations that fuel the challenges,

activities, and feedback should become as similar as possible to what will really be encountered. CCAF components should be complete, with their typical ambiguities, sporadic availability of resources, noise, interruptions, or whatever is typical.

C9-b). Vary contexts. When building general skills and knowledge to be transferred to many situations, it's important to provide a variety of contexts to demonstrate the wide applicability and utility of the skills being learned. Contexts should be interesting to the ages and lifestyles of the learners and also clearly show the empowerment provided by what is being learned.

C9-c). Don't play generic games. *Jeopardy* and *Wheel of Fortune* are fun games, but the context is the game itself. Using them as a learning context, as so many do, provides an authentic context only if you're preparing to be a contestant on one of these games. It's important

GENERIC GAMES	DONE THIS BEFORE	QUIZ ME AGAIN
$200	$200	$200
$400	$400	$400
$600	$600	$600

I'll take Generic Games for $200 please.

to use a context that matches the expected arena of performance.

Challenge

C10. Be reasonable, but don't be a softy.

C10-a). Ramp up challenges.
Challenges should generally be those that will actually be encountered in the context presented. While it's typical to make initial challenges unrealistically simple, it's much better to search out and use actual situations that happen to present the simpler challenges. This helps maintain fidelity, which, in turn, helps learners understand the value of what they're learning. Challenges can and should become more dif-

ficult, of course, while maintaining authenticity throughout the sequence.

C11. Let challenges arise from learner mistakes.

C11-a). Apply the domino effect.
With the increasing power of our software tools, it's finally become more reasonable to let learners traverse poorly chosen paths for long enough that they can experience the consequences of their mistakes rather than just receive an immediate judgment *Sorry, that's wrong. At this point you should choose. . . .* Going just a step further, if you can, allow new challenges to arise that not only reveal a previous mistake, but give learners an opportunity to make

**Your placement of the supports could be better.
Please try again.**

things better (if that's possible) by meeting subsequent challenges. Since we often have opportunities in life to correct mistakes and move on, such opportunities in e-learning may represent the ultimate authenticity and situational fidelity.

Activity

C12. Don't skip over practicalities.

C12-a). If you have to do it, you have to do it. Make it necessary to actually perform steps that would be necessary. If you'd have to go to the lab to obtain supplies, call the marketing department to procure product literature, get financial data to make a presentation, or stock specific foods for your restaurant, help learners visualize the location, the means of doing these things, and the time that will be required. Of course, we would rarely want to involve all the minute steps required nor take the actual amount of time required, but being aware of these necessities and the means of accomplishing them can be important to making the experience feel real and helping the students think about

the application of their learning as they are learning.

C12-b). Show it. As much as possible, make activities visual. Instead of a button labeled "fire the greenware," let learners drag unfired pottery to a kiln. To teach safety, you might actually make them set the greenware down first before they can open the kiln. You get the "picture."

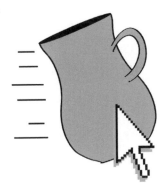

Feedback

C13. Consequences, judgments, explanations—of these, the greatest is consequences.

C13-a). Be consequential. The easiest feedback is to provide learners a judgment statement. *Yes, that's correct. No, you'll need to try again.* Actually, there's an even easier one that's worse yet. For all interactions, you can give exactly the feedback regardless of response correctness: *The correct answer is _____. Click next to go on.* The best feedback is to continually show the consequences of the learner's sequence of responses, augmented by explanation.

When to give the explanation is a bit of an open question.

If you give explanations at every step, you can condition learners not to think much about their choices. They'll select or input any convenient choice just to read the explanation. This short-circuits deeper thought and personal evaluation of performance, although it depends on how much and the type of explanation you give. In general, it's often better to wait until either success or irreversible failure has been achieved.

C13-b). Don't always make consequences obvious. Sometimes you have to seek feedback in real life to know what effect you're having. To make experiences authentic, you may want to require learners to take extra steps to gather data and evaluate their own performance, especially if that will be necessary in real life. Require them to click a photo of a manager and request feedback. Have them click the CFO's door to receive a financial report. Have them disassemble a product to be sure their crew assembled it properly.

C14. Consider how authentic you want to be.

C14-a). Let feedback be misleading! Yes, strange to say, but in the real world, feedback is often misleading. People want to be kind and will often tell us we're doing better than we are. Sometimes a bad decision works out well—talk about misleading feedback! Sometimes the best solution requires breaking a rule. Immediate feedback, in real life, might very well suggest we change course, but if we hang in there, we might be rewarded by superior success.

We have to cope with confusing feedback in real life and learn to cope with it effectively. If we want to be authentic and help learners cope, we'll sometimes want to introduce a similar lack of reliability in the feedback learners receive—at least the feedback that arrives in terms of consequences. If done well, by the way, true-to-life feedback can increase the level of intrigue considerably and create learning experiences that will drive water-cooler discussions for months.

What feedback you give and how you give it will determine much of the situational fidelity and therefore the strength of skills learned.

Michael's Misleading Feedback Experience

One of the best examples of how misleading feedback can produce a meaningful and memorable learning experience was when, after years of developing PLATO courseware and system software, I was required to take a PLATO-delivered course as part of my own management training. It included training on giving employees appropriate raises and salary adjustments.

After learning how to rank the value of employee contributions and assigning appropriate percentage salary increases, we had exercises to submit compensation plans for approval. In each practice scenario, we had to submit a proposed salary adjustment for each reporting employee. The total dollar amount needed to be within the company's annual budget for salary increases.

Try as I would, I could not find a way to fairly reward the contributions of all employees and yet not exceed the total budgeted increase for the department. I worked and reworked allocations, yet the feedback kept telling me that I was giving raises beyond the budget. I tried meeting the budget constraint, but then always found I wasn't rewarding one or more individuals properly. I could submit a request without proper rewards and see what happened or I could allocate proper rewards and exceed budget. I did the latter.

What really surprised me was that my recommended allocations were accepted with accolades for a job well done! Feedback for that exercise pointed out that, on occasion, the right thing to do for individuals will sometimes exceed departmental budgets and other times not require the entire budget available. It was important to do the right thing for individuals and work out the consequences with higher-level management.

I can remember this lesson today as clearly as I could the day I took this e-learning course over thirty years ago! And what made it so memorable is that the feedback that kept pointing out "Total Budget Exceeded" made me review and analyze my work repeatedly to be sure I wasn't making a mistake. Excellent design from our extraordinary instructional designer, Ted Martz.

Summary

So many learning events, regardless of delivery medium, ignore the importance of establishing a powerful connection with learners. If the focus is simply on the content, it's difficult to engage the full person that the learner is. Only partially engaged, learners are only able to learn part of what they could. And if the focus isn't on the learner's performance, then the outcome performance will be less than what it could have been.

Relevance, personalization, humanization, dramatic impact, authenticity, and situational fidelity are all means of bringing the learner front and center. They are means of helping learners fully engage in learning experiences that can help them realize their potential.

5 | E Is for Empower

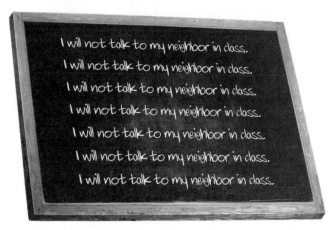

OK, so I was a pretty good student in grade school. I had to be. My mother had been a teacher, although she was not teaching when I was a student. My grandmother was on the school board through my grade school years, as was my mother when I was in high school. My dad was a city councilman, president of the Chamber of Commerce, a well-known businessman, and well known to the public of our small town. It was impressed upon me that I should be a model student.

But I was a pretty active kid and curious. It was hard for me to sit still and harder yet to be quiet. I needed to be making things, taking things apart, and generally busy. I talked a lot. No. I talked all the time.

So it would be that on too many evenings, once even when our family was invited for dinner with friends, I would be with notepaper and pencil writing such things as, "I will not talk to my neighbor in class" hundreds of times. My mother absolutely flush with embarrassment. Broken sentences of explanation. My dad doing his best to keep a straight face lest he suffer greater punishment than mine, throwing me a dutiful scowl now and then, just for insurance.

This was a while ago, of course, but there remains in my generation and many others a legacy of the axiom even today that learners should sit still, be quiet, and learn. How about, "Get busy, dig in, ask questions, talk, and learn?" What?

Designing for Doers

Designing interfaces for people who will be busy doing things to learn is quite different from designing for passive listeners. For passive listeners, we preset the agenda, order topics, sprinkle in examples, and strive for clarity. When we design for active learners, we think about how things relate to each other in multiple ways, creating learner-controlled and individualized navigation, reporting position and progress, and providing the means for direct manipulation, experimentation, and interaction.

When we think of interface design generally, we think of two things: displayed information and controls. Displayed information might be the current temperature setting on a thermostat, the speed of the car, the radio channel, or a selection from an e-learning course menu. The information helps users understand the current situation and recognize options available to them, raise or lower the temperature, turn the heat on or off, etc. Controls enable user input and can take many forms, such as levers, buttons, dials, sliders, or hyperlinks.

With mechanical devices, the position of the control is often also the display. Consider a door lock, the toaster lever, or a light switch. With electronic devices, controls are generally all methods of data input that have no mechanical function directly related to the controlled process. Instead of changing the

value of an electrical current resister to change the level of illumination, electronic controls only send input signals to a computer that changes the illumination. The difference is important because controls and displays are not automatically linked in electronic devices. Interface design must be sure to create the illusion of such linkages if they are to exist at all and assist users.

So it is with e-learning that we display information to inform learners about current situations, we alert them to input devices, controls, and options they have, and we enable their input through various gestures. Displays and controls are symbiotic and integrated in real time—or at least they should be—but this has to be done deliberately by designers and developers; otherwise, it doesn't happen. And little things matter a lot. It's frustrating to adjust a dial, for example, and not be able to see at what point you've set it until you release it. The display needs to change in concert with the movement of the dial. In many cases, we'd actually like even more advanced integration—for example, we'd like a preview of what would happen if we made a change before we disrupted the current situation or made a commitment to the prospective input.

Thankfully, new tools are on the horizon that make all of this very much easier to do. With Zebra Zapps™ technology, for example, it's almost a 95 percent design task, and only a 5 percent implementation effort. Anyone can do it.

This topic of information display and user input brings us to some of the more complicated LID issues about which there are strong opinions and more than a little research.

For example:

> **The text/narration triad:** Should text be narrated? Should narration occur alone without on-screen text? Should text appear without narration?

> **Should processes be animated?** Or are still process illustrations better? When does animation actually help?

> **How long should learning sessions be?** There are polls taken on this every so often. I kid you not.

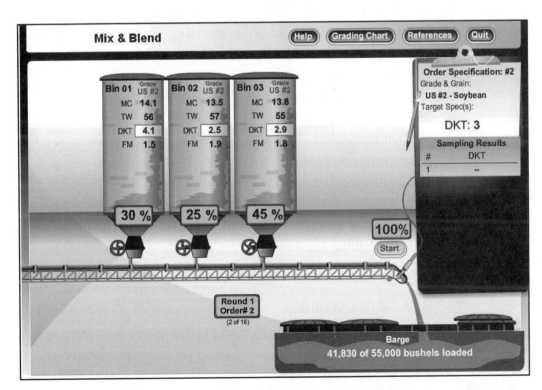

In the exercise above, the user must adjust the grain bin valve wheels to properly supply the mixture percentages of grain grades to meet the customer order.

We'll take on these issues, in context (of course), when we look at examples. In this chapter, we're going to look at two primary areas of LID:

1. Designing for visual clarity. Because we can communicate so rapidly with learners through visual means and can exceed the speed of understanding achieved through text, visual clarity is extremely important throughout the learning experience.

2. Designing input and control. e-Learners get to do everything! (If we let them.) It's not just the "lucky" person called on by the teacher who gets to experience things first-hand; it's all learners. This is perhaps the greatest benefit of e-learning, but there's more. e-Learning also provides the unique opportunity for every learner to be treated as the only learner, receiving all the attention and having everything adjusted to fit.

The process of individualizing the experience is determined to a large extent by our ability to listen to the learner, observe and evaluate performance, and make appropriate adjustments. It all begins with

identifying learner behavior. Here, unfortunately, the technology is limited in comparison to what a human can observe, so it's important to squeeze out and use available capabilities as effectively as possible.

Alternatively, learners can be given direct control over such variables as the speed, sequence, and topics of study. But even here, for learner control, the designer (and developer) must evoke or build the necessary controls. The technology is there to enable a wide range of controls with the partnering information display, but design issues are plentiful.

Visual Clarity

Less is more.

That's so much of what needs to be said. With the power of tools to provide textures to every display element, pulsate buttons, spin logos, and put an unlimited number of graphic elements all on the screen at the same time, there's a temptation to bombard learners with too much visual stimulation. With increasing clutter, selected elements must speak even louder to break through the noise. The competition escalates, and applications end up screaming at learners, who become deaf to it all, miss key points, and may even wonder what they're supposed to be doing.

The designer's job is to resist the temptation to do too much visually, to make messages clear, and help learners feel confident that they are not only aware of everything that's on the screen, but also focusing on the critical elements.

Visual Clarity
Viewed Through CCAF

Providing context, challenge, action controls, and feedback is typically done visually or at least with visual components. Much of the conversation with learners is nonverbal, even in applications dealing with language arts, as learner eyes scout out the terrain to determine what's important and what's not. Just as it's important to structure text to communicate effectively, it's important to use visual expressions well.

How can we visually communicate most effectively with learners? Again we analyze design through the CCAF lens for guidelines to achieving visual clarity:

Context
E1. Be visual.

E1-a). Trim the text. People don't

read on-screen text with accuracy. They comprehend less from on-screen text than they do from print. Use minimal amounts of text, keep the font large enough to read comfortably, and use it in support of graphics wherever possible. Better yet, skip the text and use audio to describe visuals.

E1-b). Don't fight. A red sweater stands out if the crowd isn't wearing a lot of red. But if every-

thing is red, everything fights for attention and nothing stands out. Don't use busy backgrounds and don't put everything in busy frames; just let the primary visual objects take the honors and make everything else stand down.

E2. Maintain space and place.

E2-a). Don't erase the full screen unless you are jumping to a com-

pletely different context. Add
and remove items as needed,
drawing as much or little attention in the process as is appropriate. When the screen erases,
learners have to reset themselves
too. They have to reexamine
everything on the screen to
determine whether it is a new
thing or something that was
there before. This is a disruption;
so stay put as much as possible.

**E2-b). Separate out-of-context
items from in-context items.**
Buttons for accessing help,
additional examples, progress
information, menus, and so on
are not part of the instructional
context (the bank teller's counter,
the call center, the new accounting software, the hospital room).
They should be set apart, probably kept in standard places, and,
to maintain inertia, remain visible
from event to event even when
deactivated.

**E2-c). Be consistent in the use
of space.** You increase focus,
decrease distraction, and reduce
effort for the learner when you
establish permanent places for different types of things. However,
(see next item). . .

**E2-d). Put related things
together.** Although keeping
things in standard places helps
learners know where to look for
what they want, it's even more
important to have related things
in close proximity. Horizontal
alignment is usually perceived
as closer than vertical alignment
(that is, put text and graphics side
by side rather than one over the
other).

E3. Make learning easier by eliminating distractions.

**E3-a). Avoid extraneous text,
graphics, animation, and audio.**
Learners must focus, focus, focus.
A clear to-the-point screen is far
better than a pretty screen that
lacks focus. Don't get cute with
things that don't add meaning.
You may be amused, but learners
will be distracted (and probably
annoyed).

E3-b). Don't box text (or other things) unnecessarily. For some reason, we seem to have a natural instinct to put text in a box. In many cases, this is unnecessary clutter and can even make text harder to read. Boxes in general take up precious space. Eliminating them often makes displays more inviting and less form-like. If you don't have a strong justification for a box or another form of divider, don't use one.

E3-c). Choose speech or text, but don't use both simultaneously. It would seem that use of two media to present the same message would provide helpful redundancy. But learners almost can't prevent themselves from comparing the two as they are presented, rather than thinking about the content. This is a distraction to be avoided. Speech has the distinct advantage of taking up no display space, but may be too fast or slow for the individual. It is difficult to select and review distinct passages, although controls can be provided to help.

Notice the significant improvement achieved by removing the box from the text.

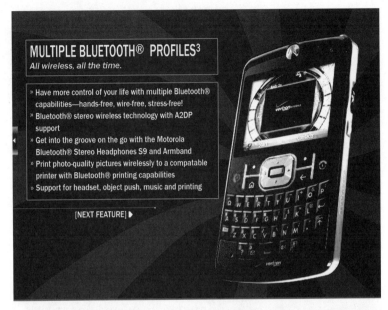

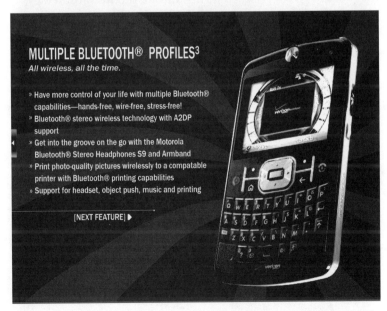

Screen captures courtesy of Motorola, Inc.

Challenge

E4. Present the challenge in context.

E4-a). Speak to the learner through the context. Challenges should build on an established context (which further strengthens the context). If you're teaching customer service, let the challenge be expressed by a customer. If you're teaching automotive repair, play the concerning sounds heard when the car is started. If teaching bank fraud, show fraudulent checks.

E4-b). Use images of people. They can be pictures, drawings, or even cartoons or sketches, but humanizing the challenge makes it more personally and psycholog-

ically engaging. A short video clip of a person reporting a problem to be solved can express not only the nature of the problem but also its importance in a very clear and impressive way. In general, photographic realism has much greater impact than illustrated figures.

Activity

E5. Differentiate controls from displays.

E5-a). Allow direct manipulation of contextual objects. The screen can actually be cleaner and simpler if controls don't have to be added for moving objects. Allow repair technicians to turn knobs and flip switches directly, rather than having to use a button to turn volume up, another to turn volume down, another to connect a speaker wire, and so on.

E5-b). Don't underline text unless it's a hyperlink. Not only does it look bad, but it's also a symbol for a hyperlink. Even if it is a link, you might use other means of differentiation to avoid the ghastly appearance of underscored text on the screen. Actually, how about never underlining text? Good idea.

Screen capture courtesy of Commission on Peace Officer Standards and Training

E5-c). Give buttons and headings distinctive appearances that cannot be confused with each other. This shouldn't have to be pointed out, and yet the practice of making them look alike is perplexingly common.

E5-d). Invite action. When the mouse cursor rolls over objects that can be manipulated, visually invite action and indicate what kind of action can be taken (click, drag in one direction, etc.). See the table on page 80 for an example of this guideline.

Feedback

E6. Use contextual elements to compose feedback.

E6-a). Display intrinsic feedback within context. The consequence of choices and actions is the feedback of situations and events. Learning is, in large part, becoming able to associate specific consequences with preceding situations and actions or inactions. So don't say, *"Good, your mixture of hydrogen peroxide and phenyl oxalate ester will glow."* Make it glow!

E7. If the feedback isn't intrinsic, create a unique visual identity for it.

E7-a). Provide mentorship in the form of an advisor. Betty Crocker, Mavis Beacon, and Aunt Jemima instilled trust in products from consumers for decades. These were fictitious personas—made-up names and images. Going as far as an avatar isn't necessary, but providing a named, pictured mentor can help learners accept and reflect on situations comfortably, while easily distinguishing between intrinsic feedback and explanatory information.

E7-b). Display judgmental feedback in a distinctive fashion, such as using an overlay with a drop shadow, a unique font and/or font color, or a unique border. The feedback should be displayed in close proximity to either the action taken, the consequences, or preferably both.

Input and Control

An appropriate complaint from many learners, whether using e-learning or attending instructor-led classes, is that they feel victimized or treated like children. If you can only look at the one screen designated for use now, if you must answer a question that might not make sense to you, if you have to keep your eyes on your own paper, if you can't talk to a fellow learner—yes, you are going to feel controlled and victimized. You are. You don't like being treated like a child.

Actually, children don't like such victimization either. *I will not talk to my neighbor in class.* Fortunately, it's neither necessary nor effective to be controlling and restrictive. Why not let learners learn?

Empower learners by giving them input and control. Let them size things up before they dig in. Let them try exercises repeatedly, if they'd like. Allow them to back up to review or explore. It's not so hard with today's technology. What might be the most difficult part, as a designer, is relinquishing total control and sharing the larger part with learners.

Of course, as with all design aspects, there is a need for balance.

Neither dizzying arrays of overwhelming controls nor a helpless lack of control are good. Finding the right place in the middle—that's the challenge.

No Control

Lecture-hall presentations, long-running videos, and even blocks of scrolling text are designed for a passive receiver who really can't do much of anything except try to absorb the information—or daydream. The little bit of navigation control that might be available in these instances, such as asking the lecturer a question, pausing the video, or scrolling back up through text, doesn't allow learners to experiment and interact with the content. It doesn't provide an effective way to associate actions with consequences. It doesn't provide a good way to learn procedures, concepts, or skills. It doesn't provide practice. It does induce sleep (or conversation with your neighbor).

Boundless Control

Filling the screen with input fields and controls can quickly overwhelm learners. Of course, if what's being taught has this type of complication, it will be necessary at some point to provide much or all of it in the lessons as well. But often the provision of overwhelming controls is a result of good intentions and poor design.

How do we get it right?

Input and Control
Viewed Through CCAF

Input and control relate mostly to the action component of CCAF, of course. But actions partner with the other components to create experiences. Let's see what learner interface designers need to consider for input and control to become most effective.

Context

E8. Build response opportunities into the context.

E8-a). Prefer direct control over remote control. For example, if a photo shows a task being performed, allow learners to click on things in the photo being done correctly (or incorrectly) rather than having to select from a remote device, such as a multiple-choice list of things in the photo.

E8-b). Make concepts, procedures, and situations tangible. Exposition of content through text facilitates text responses,

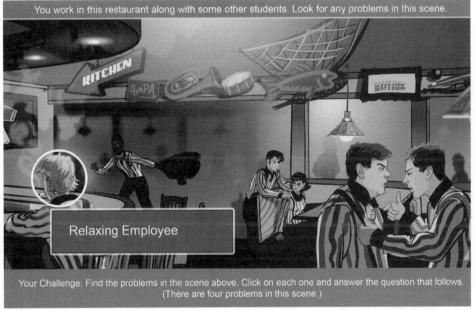

You work in this restaurant along with some other students. Look for any problems in this scene.

KITCHEN

Relaxing Employee

Your Challenge: Find the problems in the scene above. Click on each one and answer the question that follows. (There are four problems in this scene.)

Screen capture courtesy of Council on International Educational Exchange.

77

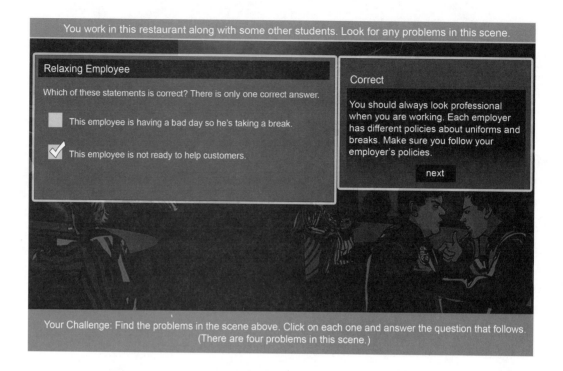

whereas visuals make the content more real and can also provide objects that learners can manipulate for more interesting response gestures and interactions.

Challenge

E9. Integrate challenges and controls.

E9-a). Use context visuals to imply the challenge and controls. For example, the image of a disassembled device with pieces randomly scattered about expresses the challenge and the controls nonverbally. Users may be uncertain about whether they need to rotate pieces to make them fit and, if so, how it is done; but with proper invitations for action, such as changing cursor shapes, learners will experiment and learn faster than through reading instructions. And they'll enjoy figuring things out more than following a set of instructions that lay it all out for them.

E10. Make challenge identification part of an action-orientated task.

E10-a). Require learners to recognize problems. Without realizing it, many learning events fail to have learners practice handling real-life scenarios because they define the problem for the learner. What may be the most critical part of successful performance is already finished and neatly served up. Present the high-level context and ask learners to probe around to determine the problem and then take steps to solve it.

Activity

E11. Empower learners with meaningful control.

E11-a). Avoid artificial restrictions. Your authoring tool or available programming skills may restrict you more than you wish, but strive not to restrict actions more than they will be restricted in real-world performance. People can typically do more than one thing at a time; so they should also do that in their e-learning experiences.

E11-b). Allow users to back up. In the real world, we can often detect mistakes we've made and correct them before someone else has to point out our errors and request correction. By delaying judgment, we're half-way there. The next task—not always an easy one to implement—is to allow learners to step back and make

corrections. This rewards learners for continuously evaluating their work—an outcome we could prize.

E12. Make control comforting and convenient.

E12-a). Don't handicap learners. One of the really great things about books is that readers are in complete control. They can skip around, read sections out of order (I read magazines back to front), reread sections, highlight sections, earmark pages, and so on. Unless you have reasons to handicap learners and make their learning tasks more difficult, why not try to give learners at least the control they have over a book.

E12-b). Make controls intuitive. The thinking we want to incite should be about the content challenge. Requiring unnecessarily complicated gestures in order to respond diverts learners from productive thinking to thinking about the interface. As instructional challenges increase in difficulty, try not to make interface complexity also increase any more than necessary.

E13. Invite action.

E13-a). Signal possible actions clearly. It's important to let learners know what objects are interactive so they won't overlook input options and controls you've given them.

Techniques for inviting action fall into the general area of user interface design (as opposed to the special topic of learner inter-

face design we're addressing in this book), but note should be made that interactions as seemingly simple as drag and drop provide a surprisingly long list of action invitation possibilities. Consider these:

Drag and Drop User Interface

Condition	Invitation	Example	
On mouse over	Indicate movability and invite "mouse down."	Change cursor shape when over a movable object.	
On mouse down	Invite drag.	Shadow object to visually lift it above others. Hide cursor so moving mouse moves object.	
When object is near position of origin	Inform that release will cancel drag action.	Highlight position of origin. Object snaps back to origin on release.	

Drag and Drop User Interface

Condition	Invitation	Example
When object has been placed in an invalid posiition	Invite repositioning.	Ghost object.
When object is near a valid target	Invite drop.	Erase position of origin.
When object is on a valid target	Confirm success.	Snap to exact position. Remove shadow. Add sound effect.

Feedback

E14. Make states clear.

E14-a). Communicate progress honestly.

Checking off menu items or showing a progress bar is helpful to learners who need to schedule their time and meter their energy. Menus and progress bars work well if items are of similar difficulty and duration. If they're not, they can be quite inaccurate measures. Indicate relative proportions when variation is significant:

Unit Progress

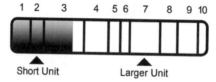

Short Unit   Larger Unit

E14-b). Show the current state clearly.

A design disaster found with bewildering frequency comes from confusing the display of a current state with the function of a button to change to another state.

Does this button/indicator tell me that I'm _in_ play mode or that the video _is_ paused? If it is indicating I'm in play mode, then it will probably look like a play button when I'm paused. This reversal of states and operations can become very confusing and is easily avoidable.

Similarly, does the illustration below tell me that I responded incorrectly to the first and second

Meaningful measures of instructional effectiveness are:

☒ Ability to perform learned skills several weeks after training.

☐ Ability to perform learned skills immediately after training.

☒ Number of learners passing the course.

☐ Number of response errors made during training.

answers and correctly to the third? Or does it tell me I was correct to have chosen the first but should also have chosen the second and not the third? It can be hard to see the ambiguity if you know the content well, but this common, "compact" feedback method can be very confusing to learners.

Summary

Learning has to be done by learners themselves. Adult learners, while they don't always choose the best activities to help themselves, don't like to be constrained. When learners are disgruntled from being treated like children, an otherwise optimal learning event may not be very effective. But given controls and the ability to receive advice, adult learners may be comforted by having control and take advantage of all an e-learning application has to offer.

In any case, e-learning provides the unique opportunity for all learners to be doers. Empowered by e-learning, every learner can experience the interactivity you provide, gaining from the experience and practice exercises in preparation for skilled performance.

6 | O Is for Orchestrate

When I was beginning to design Authorware, a visual e-learning authoring tool, a friend of mine introduced me to a retired and eccentric psychologist. The setting was just as you might expect in a movie: He lived in his office, a loft in an old industrial brick building, which was more than overflowing with books and notebooks. His thoughts jumped from topic to topic more quickly than your eyes could dart around the dimly lighted menagerie.

With no computer in sight, I began doubting he was aware of such things as authoring systems and sensed he couldn't help me evaluate our prospects for success with the new technology. A waste of time? I showed him a little authoring

by dragging icons for such things as a display, an animation, a question, anticipated responses, and feedback into a sequence. He started firing questions.

"How do adults learn?" I thought his question was a non sequitur to the demo I had given, but nevertheless relevant to the quest of developing instructional software. I took a moment to organize my thoughts. Where to start? I was, after all a Ph.D. in educational psychology, facing a broad but familiar question to which much could be said. But was this a rhetorical question or one I was really intended to take on. The quandary terminated abruptly.

"See all these books? They're important records, but not, for the most part, instructional." This point, I fully understood. I started to speak without hesitation, but it wasn't yet the time. Interrupting my insignificant concurrence, he challenged me again.

"What have you observed about how children learn?" In retrospect, I think

Яapid readeR

- Express content in condition—action—consequence statements.

- Having the opportunity to practice in an open learning space allows learners the time to actually learn, not just fill in answers on an exam at the end.

- Good challenges, overlaid on an open learning space, provide advantages of goal directedness and an exploratory environment.

this actually was when I was supposed to answer, but having repeatedly mistaken the soliloquy for a conversation, I comfortably let silence hang. Wrong.

"OK. If you're going to be successful in this learning, computing thing, you need to understand a fundamental here. Tell me this: if you give a child a toy truck, what will he do with it?" *Pleased, I think, that I hadn't managed to disrupt his play with me, a new wave of enthusiasm in his voice. It was clearly time to speak.* **"Well, a child will push the truck around and probably make a motor noise, I guess."**

"For a moment, maybe."
Delighted I had produced the expected wrong answer, he sent me off to watch children learn, but generously preempted my discovery. Children will rarely do with toys what we expect them to do. They'll rarely use them for what they're made. With a truck, he

said, they'll very quickly start pulling on the parts to see what comes off, if anything. They'll drop the truck or slam it into things to see what happens. If they like the sound, they'll repeat the action. If they can get parts off, they'll bump the parts into each other to see whether there's any interaction, stack them up, or throw them. The fact that the truck no longer operates like a truck is of no concern. They may forget or never even realize the parts were from a truck.

"Given two trucks, kids will stack them on top of each other, push one with the other, crash them into each other, and so on." *And the point?*

"Your authoring icons are like toys. And that's good because adults are basically large children and learn in the same way. They'll stack your icons up and use them in combinations you never imagined, just to see what will happen (although they'll be more restricted in their experiments than children, because they'll want to have purpose guiding them).

"You've orchestrated a fantastic place for learning—for authors to learn, that is. Now if authors can use your software to create the same kind of learning space

for their students, where they can explore, discover even more than you intended, and show you how to enrich learning environments, you will have really done something, Michael.

"Good day."

Orchestrating Learning Spaces

The primary challenge to creating effective learning is not the challenge of presenting information and doing it in ways that people will remember. The primary challenge is to create situations in which learners practice making alternative choices, experience the outcomes, come to understand the relationships between behaviors and outcomes, and apply knowledge and skill successfully. In short, the target is not to enable learners to remember things told them, but to enable learners to make desired outcomes happen.

Success comes from doing the right thing at the right time. It doesn't come from knowing what to do, but from being able to do it. It doesn't come from being able to do it and not doing it. It comes from doing the right thing at the right time.

Building well-orchestrated learning spaces is no easy task. But just understanding that such learning spaces are composed of contexts, challenges, activities, and feedback gives designers direction. Successful learning spaces are built on very well-conceived, constructed, and integrated CCAF components, as we have been discussing, and they generally have one of two forms, open or goal-oriented.

Open Learning Spaces

Open learning spaces let learners explore and pursue their own interests as they develop and change. They can be fun and intriguing because they provide extra-high levels of learner control. Learners can try things of interest and abandon them if and when interest draws them elsewhere. The fantastic interactive series, "What's the Secret?," built in conjunction with the public television series *Newton's Apple*, was an excellent example.

The menu was a hodgepodge of interesting graphics. No standard table of contents here. Each fascinating graphic was designed to draw a click, especially because sometimes what it represented was far from clear. Clicking a plane, for example,

Learners adjust the dance of a scout bee then see if they correctly reported the location and quality of flowers.

could lead to a discussion of the Doppler effect. Clicking bees delivered the opportunity to learn how to communicate with bees and test your skills to see whether they could find the flowers you were trying to direct them to.

Some open learning spaces are designed much as laboratories in which learners can create their own challenges or select from those suggested, ask for guidance if they like, and experiment to build cause-and-effect understanding. By the way, it's easy to overlay some assigned goals onto an open learning space when specific outcomes are desired.

Goal-Oriented Learning Spaces

Successful, goal-oriented learning spaces provide a sequence of learning experiences, each advancing the learner's ability toward defined performance objectives. To transfer skills from the learning space to real application, they must provide contexts, challenges, input, and controls that correspond to those learners will actually encounter or need to perform learned tasks.

Goal-oriented learning spaces are built with the same CCAF components as open learning spaces, but learner options are usually more restricted. Desing teams sometimes discover that building open learning spaces and then providing specific goals for learners to accomplish can actually simplify construction. It can also be a path to providing a richer and less restrictive learning experience—sometimes even at a lower cost. This approach is often bypassed because it initially seems that too much time and effort would be required to provide all the general facilities needed to make the space seem well rounded. But as goal-oriented learning spaces develop, there is often an increasing desire and effort to give learners more options and fuller feedback. The narrowed focus that justified the goal-oriented approach becomes restrictive and burdensome to overcome. All is not happy.

The learner interface designer should study these alternate paths early in the process of designing learning solutions.

LID Considerations for Orchestrating Successful Learning Events

In this chapter, we primarily consider goal-oriented learning spaces and look at three groups of LID considerations for orchestrating successful learning events:

1. *Build events on performance-based learning objectives.*

Some learning spaces are designed primarily for exploration and with the hope of unpredictable, but positive outcomes. But when learning applications are built for specific outcomes, it's important that targeted outcomes guide and assist both authors and learners.

2. *Construct exercises that challenge each learner and provide an opportunity for giving guidance through feedback.*

Exercises that are neither too hard nor too easy for a learner are effective. At the same time, challenges at all levels have to be interesting to keep learners focused and engaged. To achieve both, it's helpful to put challenges up-front to gauge initial learner ability, help learners meet the challenge through whatever level of feedback may prove necessary, and then select the next exercise based on measured performance.

3. *Provide the kinds of inputs and controls learners will actually be able to use in performing their tasks.*

For a theater or movie performance to work, viewers must suspend disbelief. Viewers know that

not all things they see are real, but if they are constantly reminded that we're just pretending, they can miss the message, the entertainment, and the experience as a whole. In learning experiences, if learners are cautioning themselves it isn't really like this—*my job isn't a multiple-choice question*—they'll not be able to gain useful, applicable skills.

To make things as real or authentic as possible, think in terms of establishing conditions that learners must recognize in order to select and take appropriate action. Enable the closest approximation you can to the action the learner would actually carry out, and then similarly approximate the consequences of whatever actions the learner took. In other words, think believable conditions, actions, and consequences.

1. Performance-Based Learning Objectives

I've frequently stated that presenting typical behavioral objectives to learners does little good because they make such boring reading. Learners skip over them, desiring instead to get into the course material and go through it without delay. This typical behavior doesn't mean, of course, that learners wouldn't benefit from thinking about and focusing on the purpose of learning the content at hand.

Authors need to know and remember what the purpose of a learning experience is as they create it. Learners can make the best use of their experience if they monitor their own progress against a purpose and mentally project application of new facts, concepts, procedures, and skills into their workflow. The challenge then is to continually and effectively reflect and communicate the objectives through as many components of learning events as possible.

Performance-Based Learning Objectives
Viewed Through CCAF

Context

O1. Think theater. Think experience. Be dramatic.

O1-a). Create tension to communicate objectives. Objectives typically have a boring, sterile, academic tone to them. Instead of listing behavioral objectives that few learners read, let the context communicate the objectives by showing a problematic situation—a disaster, layoffs, lost sale, unhappy customers, etc.

O1-b). Don't give the outcome away. Who would want to go to a movie that began by saying, "Here's what's going to happen, watch for this, and expect this outcome"? This is what many learning designs do, and this is what kills the possibility of a great and authentic learning experience.

Challenge

O2. Think role playing.

O2-a). Put the learner in the story. The objective can be very clear when you are given an assignment to perform. It makes the experience much more direct

than simply learning to list the principles of good performance.

O2-b). Switch roles. By giving learners various roles to play, they can come to understand alternate perspectives and more deeply understand dynamics or processes. For example, if you're teaching customer service, let the learners play the role of an unhappy customer. They'll actually gain a deeper sense of why learning effective skills is important.

O2-c). Let the learner mentor. Sometimes learners can be more reflective and sometimes more exploratory when another character is performing a task, subject to guidance from the learner. If the character is failing to remember and/or perform certain steps, the learner as mentor can become acutely aware of how important specific learning and performance tasks are.

Activity

O3. Provide realistic distractions and confusion.

O3-a). Make objectives real. Even though words describing situations and conditions may be there in the objective (but often aren't), *at a typical airline ticket*

counter, it's easy to set aside the real-life impact of a statement about the performance environment and concentrate simply on learning how to do things. Handling a noisy environment, with frequent interruptions and constantly changing priorities, may actually prove to be the toughest aspect of the learning task. Activities the learner performs must therefore encounter these same kinds of performance disruptions.

O3-b). Match activities to objectives. Although it makes sense to simplify activities for new learners so they can focus, avoid confusion, and not face overwhelming obstacles, it's easy for activity design to completely overturn critical aspects of objectives. Multiple-choice structures, for example, too often switch from an activity that should require recall or problem solving into much simpler and unrealistic recognition activity.

Feedback

O4. Compare performance to objectives.

O4-a). Chart progress against proficiency (not content). People want to know where they are within a module or course. They often think in terms of how many more pages, chapters, or hours they have yet to go. But those measures substitute the objective of "getting through this" for the intended objective of mastery, skill-building, and competence. So chart proficiency as a measure of progress to help learners keep focused on the real objectives.

O5. Stay in character.

O5-a). Again, stay visual and authentic. Show the outcome rather than describing it, whenever possible. Will feedback in actual poor performance situations come simply as someone's neat, tidy, and respectful verbal assessment, or will people get mad? They'll probably get mad. Will an assembly line shut down? Will the sales team lose a bonus? Will the patient have months of recovery instead of days?

2. Challenge and Help

There's so much benefit to kicking off with a challenge. *Right off the bat, here's a situation. Can you handle it, learner? If you struggle, we're here to help! Explore, take the lead, have fun. It's really all about you.*

If the challenge is an interesting one (it had better be), if the learner can understand it (we need to know our audience and the range of reasonable expectations), and if meeting the challenge would have personal value (it shouldn't be here if it doesn't), we're going to realize important benefits from orchestrating this type of learning event. Among the benefits are:

➤ Learners will instantly know what the course is about. They don't have to wait until reaching the post-test or final exam to know for sure.

➤ Learners will be engaged and active. We didn't take the energy and curiosity they may have had when they arrived and turn it off by putting them in a passive listening or reading mode.

➤ We'll have an opportunity to assess the individual's abilities at the earliest possible moment.

➤ We'll be able to more accurately set the level of the second and subsequent challenges for each individual learner because we will have sampled some of his or her skills.

Afraid to Challenge?

Are you afraid of presenting challenges learners can't meet? Are you afraid they'll be frustrated and quit? Don't be. It's actually OK if you present an initial challenge that is somewhat over the heads of learners. It's often a good thing. Really. Here's why:

➤ First, look again at the list of benefits above. If you present the challenge in the right way (and there are a few rules), learners will recognize the benefits and work with you.

➤ Second, a challenge that learners can't meet expresses the outcome objectives; that is, *this is the very type of challenge you will be able to meet when you've completed your learning.* It gives learners something to anticipate and look forward to. Do you want to learn the piano so you can play "Twinkle, Twinkle, Little Star"? Really? What about "Maple Leaf Rag"? The reason to learn Twinkle, Twinkle, of course, is to build the skills you need for "Maple Leaf Rag." But let's get real. We're going for "Maple Leaf Rag."

There's no competition between presenting a challenge that's too difficult for learners and not presenting a challenge at the beginning. The up-front challenge wins. So put aside your fears and give it a try. But do it after studying the tips below so that you'll do it in an effective way.

Viewing Challenge and Help Through CCAF

Context

O6. Make a good first impression.

O6-a). Establish broad appeal. We may not know much about the individual yet, but learners begin sizing us up instantly. *Am I going to get anything useful out of this?* So, instead of starting with something bland, start with popular content in a context that has compelling components that are easy to relate to.

O6(b). Get into it quickly. Look for an initial context and challenge that are easy to grasp. There are so many ways to delay getting learners active, and all of them risk putting learners into a passive mode. So, especially at the outset, try for a context and challenge that don't require extensive explanation.

Challenge

O7. Pop the challenge.

O7-a). Ready, fire, aim. While it's not always a good strategy to "just do something," it's definitely not a good idea to delay putting the challenge on the table. Don't precede the challenge with lots of orientation, instructions, qualifiers, or other detail, even if you have to go back later to provide more details about the context upon which the challenge is based.

O8. Instill a sense of confidence.

O8-a). Not too easy or too hard. Too easy is better than too hard, but getting it about right is best. There is leeway, and by supplying proper help and feedback, you can move all learners comfortably through initial challenges until you can adjust the challenge level so that less exhaustive support is necessary.

Especially as learners are first becoming comfortable with the way you have orchestrated the learning events, you want them to quickly gain a sense of confidence that they can both work the interface mechanics well and meet the learning challenges. You want

them eagerly looking forward to the next challenge.

Game designers know how important this is and work to make sure new users have a string of successes before letting the challenge level ramp up. If, on the other hand, the challenges are too easy, users may decide the application isn't worth their time. LIDers face the same test as game designers.

O8-b). Provide a worked example. Worked examples have shown exceptional instructional power, but unless learners have a problem of their own to work, reviewing worked examples can be yet another way of delaying activity and putting learners in a passive mode. So go ahead and present the challenge, but provide access to one or more similar reference challenges together with step-by-step explanations of their solutions.

O8-c). Be ready with graduated help. But don't help too much. This may be the trickiest part. You want to respond to the learner's request for help, but you don't want to provide a shortcut that makes thinking unnecessary. If it's true that the purpose of human life is to find the shortest path between any two points, it's true that learners will take the easiest path they can find. If it's to request help because help reveals answers easily, learners will request help without facing your challenges at all. One solution is to give only hints rather than answers. Going further, you can require learners to make effortful attempts to answer after receiving each hint before another will be offered, thus making it easier to actually attempt solutions rather than to repeatedly request help.

O8-d). Mix levels. Don't continually make challenges harder. Mix in some easier ones for practice and review, including some really easy ones just to remind learners how much progress they've made. Mixing challenge levels increases fun and interest.

O8-e). Power up. The strengths that learners acquire should empower them. At some point, reward progress by giving achievers extra capabilities, such as auto completion of simple or preparatory tasks that have been thoroughly mastered. Learners will appreciate being given partial solutions and find them very rewarding.

Every once in a while, you'll want to return to having learners practice all levels of tasks as a means of spaced practice, but "power ups" are greatly appreciated rewards that fight boredom and also allow learners to focus on specific new skills.

O8-f). Offer control. It's rewarding and motivating to be given the reins, to be allowed to steer. As learners progress, consider giving them more and more control. It's perhaps a form of "power up," but control can include such

options as deciding for yourself whether to practice more now and push for progress later or try moving up right away and practice later.

Activity

O9. Give users options.

O9-a). Allow "studying up." Concurrent with giving learners challenges they may not be prepared to meet, it's important to provide effective and reassuring support. It's smart to avoid the tradition of explaining everything to learners first and asking them to understand and remember it all until they finally apply it. But that doesn't mean you should intentionally withhold information. Have good help, such as demonstrations, guides, worked examples, and full reference documentation, available for when learners ask for it. Allow learners to pause interactions without penalty in order to study.

O9-b). Allow "do-overs." We've observed that with many of our best-designed interactions, learners want the opportunity to do them over. Why? Because, quite commonly, in the first "do-over" learners want to confirm for

themselves that they can do much better, if not perfectly. In the second "do-over" (yes, forget that simplistic and erroneous notion that learners want and will only accept 5-to-15-minute learning sessions; they may suffer poor designs for only a very short time, but with good ones, learners aren't always looking for a quick exit), learners will do something very, very smart: They will intentionally experiment with wrong answers to see what happens. This exploration can yield many great learning moments.

O9-c). Allow previewing. Who doesn't skim through a book to get a sense of its contents, length, and style? Even online booksellers have found it important to allow buyers to browse through books before purchasing.

O10. Provide assistance.

O10-a). Be there. Although you can't physically be there for learners, your presence can be felt if you provide support and help. As learners work to meet challenges, sense when help is needed and offer it. Think about offering help after a string of poor responses, frequent use of links to reference materials without interleaved correct responses, long delays between responses, and so on.

O10-b). Don't penalize use of help. In many contexts, asking for help requires taking some risk. *Does it reveal that I'm not prepared or paying attention? Maybe I shouldn't admit I'm confused. It might go on my record.* Unless it's a certification or evaluation exercise, we want learners to ask for help. Don't penalize them for doing so. However, (see next point). . .

Feedback

O11. Provide "power up" tips.

O11-a). Be a generous tipper. Because we don't want to expound content before learners become active and because we want intrinsic feedback to reveal results of learner activities, we have limited opportunities to provide tips and ancillary information. When learners ask for information or flounder, there's no problem. We can always provide additional information when requested. But if learners succeed without such help, don't forget to tip anyway: speak up at the point of transition from one event to another, providing learners the

opportunity to replay the previous challenge and test out the advantages of your tips. Explanations can round out learners' knowledge and help them understand why certain behaviors produce results they want.

O11-b). Don't give away too much. Just as help can yield so much information that learners can figuratively or even literally cut and paste answers without thinking, feedback can do the same thing. In some designs, learners can enter any random response to receive feedback that eventually reveals the correct answer. So that's what learners do.

3. Performance-Relevant Input and Control

If this, then that. Called production rules by intelligent systems designers, if-then statements can be used to describe how the world works.

> ➤ If you drop a cup, then it will fall to the ground.
> ➤ If you don't understand product capabilities, then you can't recommend the appropriate product.
> ➤ If you have lost your Internet connection, then e-mail messages

you attempt to send will accumulate in your Outbox folder.

Learning how to do things involves internalizing valid production rules. *If I put the eggs and bacon on to cook at the same time, then the eggs will be done cooking long before the bacon is ready. If I hold down the shift key, then I can select multiple objects.*

Production rules can help learner interface designers identify and focus on content that is of the most importance for learning effective skills and behavior. This is because production rules stress connections between **actions** *if this is done* and **consequences** *then this will happen.* They identify inputs, responses, or actions that will need to be enabled, recognized, and judged, and they identify associated consequences that

can become intrinsic feedback.

In fact, if we elaborate the structure just a bit, breaking it into the three components of conditions, actions, and consequences, it provides an excellent way of boiling overwhelming volumes of instructional content down to the critical components. It also provides an excellent way of restating content in concise terms. Not bad, huh?

Condition, Action, Consequence

If-then statements are often easier to use for learner interface design purposes when the if component is broken into two components, *conditions* and *actions*.

➤ *If* the cup is ceramic and three or more feet above the floor (condition), dropping it (action) will cause it to break (consequence).

➤ *If* the customer has made a previous purchase from us (condition), asking about his or her experience with it before suggesting additional purchases (action) gives you an opportunity to build rapport (consequence).

➤ *If* the employee's poor performance has not been documented and discussed with the employee (condition), penal-

99

izing the employee (action) may lead to an actionable complaint (consequence).

A primary purpose of learner input capabilities and controls is to help people experiment with condition-action-consequence relationships, learn them, and apply them. Undertaking content analysis from this perspective prepares you to create your contexts, challenges, activities, and feedback. It gives you an excellent foundation for orchestrating your learning events.

Performance-Relevant Input and Control
Viewed Through CCAF

Context

O12. Create conditions with the "if" gradually becoming more subtle from one exercise to the next.

> **O12-a). Elementary, my dear Watson.** Scrutinizing the context for the critical "if" conditions is almost always the first step toward successful performance. Learners need to become skilled in recognizing the conditions—a learning and performance objective that's

often overlooked. At first, conditions should be clear so learners can identify them. But as skills develop, they should become less obvious to provide practice on investigating conditions.

> **O12-b). Match media to real-world sources.** If some information is available only in spreadsheets, in charts, in textual documents, through discussion or other forms of communication and resources, select media that most directly match the sources learners will need to use.

> **O12-c). Hide what's hidden.** If real performance contexts have information that must be sought out, extracted, or constructed, and learners will actually have to do this to perform well, we want them practicing these skills in their e-learning. So if critical information is often hidden,

require learners to take steps to uncover it, to ask necessary questions, or even fill out requisition forms.

O12-d). Facilitate multiple challenges. It takes time to become familiar with a context. If just one context can host multiple problems and performance conditions, learners will be able to get more practice from a less costly e-learning application.

O12-e). Invite alternative actions. There's little to be learned from a context that puts forth only one condition the learner can respond to. Set up multiple conditions with multiple possible actions.

O12-f). Supply incorrect information. If it happens that information is sometimes incorrect and it's important to corroborate information before acting, provide incorrect information without being obvious about it. Give learners realistic means of validating information.

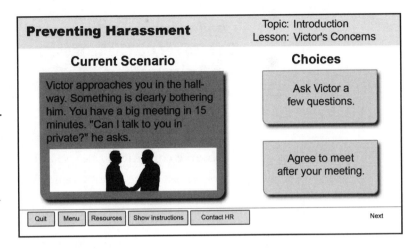

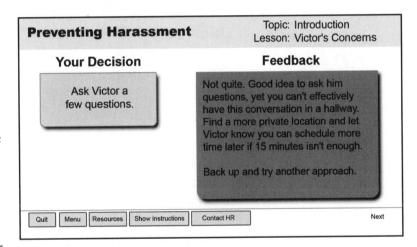

Learners are acting as a manager who is approached by an employee with a sexual harassment concern. In this context, the learner must repeatedly select from the multiple possible actions that determine how the encounter unfolds.

Challenge

O13. To set up challenges, familiarize learners with the conditions, actions, and consequences individually.

O13-a). Challenge learners to observe conditions. Before learners can associate specific conditions with appropriate actions, they need to know what to look for. Have them demonstrate and/or build their abilities to discern salient aspects of conditions—even guessing if they need to.

O13-b). Familiarize learners with actions to consider. Learners need to have an idea of actions that are possible. They may not be able to guess what's possible or, at the opposite extreme, you may not be able to list all the actions that should be considered. Providing examples and clarifing whether there are either correct actions to memorize or a reference procedure to use will help prepare learners for their challenges.

O13-c). Don't give away consequences. Doing so can be like reading the last chapter of a mystery novel first. Don't take the experience out of the experience by foreshadowing consequences of alternative actions the learner can choose. You will want to state goals, such as "find the accounting error," "assign tasks to the best individuals to handle them," or "make sure the customer is satisfied before concluding the call." But don't indicate the consequences of either good or poor performance in any detail. That will reduce the impact of the subsequent consequences and feedback.

O14. Associate conditions and actions with consequences.

O14-a). Forward association. Although we don't want to spoil the power of intrinsic feedback, it can be a powerful exercise for learners to think ahead about possible consequences. Ask learners to predict what consequences would happen if they took various actions.

O14-b). Backward association. Create challenges that ask learners to explain what actions would have resulted in different consequences.

Activity

O15. Prefer controls to inputs.

O15-a). Invite exploration.
Because we're always trying to prepare learners to do valuable things, we want them busy doing things frequently in their e-learning experiences. Invite learners to be curious and adventurous. Let them become acquainted with their learning environment through exploration rather than through your painstakingly thorough explanation of everything.

O15-b). Match behavioral modalities.
If the real-world activity would require moving something, have learners drag objects. If they would have to type a message, have them type one. If they'd have to tell a caller his credit application is being denied, have them record what they would say. If they'd circle a point on a map, have them circle a point on a map. Try not to make activities either more complicated or less complicated than actual performance will require, keeping in mind that you may want to start with simplified activities and build up to greater fidelity. (See O16-b on learner readiness below.)

O16. Match controls.

O16-a). Match controls to content.
Consider the nature of the content when selecting activity modalities. Sometimes the content necessitates activity modalities that don't really represent actions learners will perform. To learn where to place seismographic equipment, for example, it's not necessary to simulate driving a truck from location to location to place seismographs. Moving icons on a map is a much better modality match.

O16-b). Match controls to learner readiness.
For complex tasks, things may need to be simplified at first. Almost everything is a candidate for simplification. Conditions can be made much simpler than any that will really be found, the choice of actions can be both restricted and

presented as a list of choices that would never actually be provided, and the controls and inputs can be simplified so that learners have fewer things to learn all at once. As learner capabilities develop, controls can become more complex and realistic to aid with transfer of learning to real-world performance.

Feedback

O17. Think consequences.

O17-a). Use intrinsic feedback. Consequences are intrinsic feedback and much more impactful than giving learners extrinsic feedback. (*Yes, that's correct!*) Showing learners what has happened because of their actions helps cement the relationships among conditions, actions, and consequences.

O17-b). Delay judgment. It's not unusual that those consequences in life that reveal the quality of our action are delayed. Meaningful consequences often don't appear until we've completed a series of actions. In many cases, parroting this real-life experience makes e-learning experiences more effective. Delays not only teach learners that they won't always receive immediate

feedback, but they also encourage learners to continuously evaluate their work and scurry around to make corrections if necessary while there may still be time.

O18. Provide mentorship.

O18-a). Check first steps. Did the learner not understand the conditions set forth in the context? In helping learners build the condition—action—consequence associations, it's important to make sure learners didn't misread the conditions and set off on the wrong path, take the wrong actions, and obtain baffling consequences. If they did go off on a tangent because of misreading conditions, provide explanation and hold their hands as you step through the solution starting with context analysis.

O18-b). Prompt beginning learners. Provide observations and assistance, perhaps through representation of a coach. Do it without giving away answers, which can cause learners to lean heavily on the coach and avoid developing independent skills. Remind learners of things to consider—not just the things they haven't considered, but a mix of both those they appear

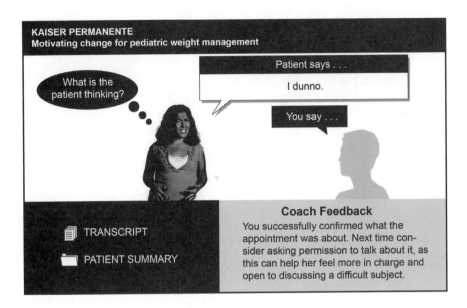

In this program designed for physicians, the learner is working through a weight management discussion with an adolescent patient. As the learner navigates through the conversation, a coach provides feedback after each decision.

Screen capture courtesy of Kaiser Permanente

to have remembered and not remembered.

O18-c). Promote exploration and initiative. Keeping experiences interesting and realistic requires some dependency on learner curiosity and willingness to explore. If learners haven't exercised controls that would be helpful, haven't tapped resources (hidden or in plain sight), or otherwise been effective in use of your learning affordances, some helpful prompts can make the experience much more effective. But avoid the temptation to use the "explain every cotton-pickin' thing" solution. It's very easy to get boring (and you know you'll want to do it). Don't.

Summary

Expressing content in condition(s)—action(s)— consequence(s) statements is a helpful and powerful way of enabling yourself, as learner interface designer, to orchestrate learning events. On this foundation, you can build either open learning spaces, designed primarily for learner exploration and serendipitous learning, or goal-oriented learning spaces comprised of context, challenge, activity, and feedback. An excellent and often cost-saving approach is to first build an open learning space and then overlay performance-based objectives along with any CCAF components that may be needed.

Part Three

Good and Bad Influences

7 | Fatal Attractions

Multiple-choice. What is the moral of the Adam and Eve story?

☐ *1. You need both hands to cover your private parts. You shouldn't try to eat at the same time.*

☐ *2. Adam and Eve's disobedience should teach us a vital lesson concerning man's limitations: Unless he adheres to divine guidance, man is prone to make wrong decisions.*

☐ *3. He who seeks knowledge and self-sustenance will be punished.*

You can select more than one answer.

As learner interface designers, we need to be careful about what is influencing our thoughts and designs and try to recognize the effect it is having on us. While we may find various designs appealing in non-learning contexts, we need to be careful about being led astray. It can happen so very easily and completely without our awareness until we end up with regrettable outcomes.

Good and Bad Influences

In this chapter, we'll review some of the primary sources of design influence that are having regrettable influence on learning interface design. While the remainder of this book emphasizes what we should

strive for as designers and how we can achieve it, in this chapter I attempt to identify negative influences and things we must try to avoid.

Presentation Design

The design of e-learning has been, for better or for worse (mostly for worse), shaped by no single medium more than PowerPoint. This is truly regrettable.

Of course, effective presentation within e-learning is important, and good design principles for presenting information, such as Tufte's

Яapid readeR

- PowerPoint and Internet applications offer many appealing interface designs that are unfortunately poisonous to learning events.

- Linear presentations, informative and transactional Web sites, general software applications, and games are all poor models for learner interface design.

109

[www.edwardtufte.com] notable works, offer much guidance for both presentations and e-learning design. Clear, graphical presentation of concepts achieved through de-emphasis of text, bullet points, clip art, and distracting transitions is certainly important for both conference talks and e-learning.

But presentations designed for a passive listening audience are not easily converted into learning experiences, no matter how attractive the notion and commonplace the attempts. To be sure, carefully constructed and organized content is expensive. Once constructed, it has become a significant investment. One wants to make multiple uses of it whenever possible. Such materials can, indeed, be useful in the construction of e-learning, as can all items that help define and clarify facts, concepts, procedures, and so on.

There is so much interest in doing this that an industry of tools has arisen to ease the "repurposing" of presentation materials for interactive courseware. Where the need is primarily to disseminate information through multiple channels, this practice meets with acceptable success often enough. But when

instruction is needed, starting from a base of content developed and organized for presentations can prove unfortunate and very problematic. Why is this?

Linearity

Presentation slides are typically organized for linear flow in concert with a speech. This organization, much like that of a book, imposes a page-turning paradigm that stunts the imagination of designers who, when they begin by working with presentation slides, often unwittingly start thinking in terms of pages, transitions, and explanations instead of experiences, actions, consequences, and, well, context, challenges, activities, and feedback (CCAF). You can clearly detect e-learning applications that had their beginnings in presentation slides in most cases. They're the boring ones.

Cellular Structure

Content must be broken into page-size pieces for presentation. This process institutes artificial content boundaries, boundaries that are too frequently built on in conversion to e-learning, becoming part of the content rather than being purged from it. While segmentation can be helpful for learning, segmentation for interactivity and learning events is very different from the arbitrary slicing of content for presentation slides. When slides are in hand, many organizations shy away from the restatement of the content needed for good interactivity. Understandable but disastrous.

Too Much Breadth—Too Little Depth

Information structured for presentation traverses a path of selected points and principles. The writer selects data and examples that support primary message points, necessarily neglecting those that will take too long to present, are too tedious or complicated for a large audience, or are too specific for broad appeal. If a question is raised during presentation, the presenter can provide more depth.

Presentations generally provide high-level information, often avoiding intricate details that are critical to actually applying and using the information. To be interactive and actually build usable skills, e-learning requires much more detailed information than a presentation holds and yet cannot usually deal with the overwhelming breadth of relatively shallow information supplied.

It's a Problem

CCAF describes what's missing in presentations and why material developed and organized for presentation does not provide essential components for e-learning design. Unless e-learning is simply being used to distribute information, presentation materials and a presentation mentality often lead to very poor learning designs.

Web Design

Web designers recognize that the user experience is critical. If visitors to a site are confused, not finding what they're looking for, or just not having a good experience, they'll leave. Perhaps it's the simple difference that presentation audiences are often trapped, whereas Web visitors are anonymous and very free to leave, that explains the very different design approaches taken for these two kinds of applications.

As in e-learning, Web sites can't afford much of a user interface learning curve. Much creative effort in Web design is focused on making situations instantly understandable, options recognizable, and interactions aligned with user expectations. When a new, effective interface mechanism is invented, it spreads widely through the Internet, appearing everywhere so as not to disappoint users, who quickly come to expect it.

Many of these designs can be employed effectively in e-learning, but as with presentations, Web sites don't have the same goals as e-learning and therefore can be false and harmful models to guide LID.

Information Access

Interactivity in Web-based interactions is designed to facilitate access to information—to yield desired information as quickly and easily as possible. Users are looking for prices, availability, comments, movie times, images, contact information, directions. In e-learning, we work to create memorable experiences. We give learners tempting opportunities to make mistakes they can learn from. The interaction and the experiences are the products we're creating, while Web sites strive to take the thinking out of interactions, making them transparent utilities for information retrieval.

In short, good Web design is more about information architecture than about meaningful, memorable, motivating user experiences. Web site user interface naturally reflects the Web site's purpose.

User Direction

Web sites are basically menu-driven applications that acquaint users as efficiently as possible with what information is available and provide access to it. Similarly, e-learners are sometimes given the driver's seat, allowing them to take the initiative to meet a specific learning need:

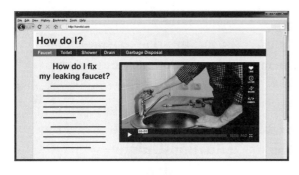

How can I fix my leaking faucet?
How can I write a good resume? How
should I make chateaubriand? Web
site design models are helpful here.

But within a content area, learners often don't know what they don't
know. They don't know what they're
looking for. Unfortunately, designers biased by Web site design forget
this and simply give learners menus
rather than creating experiences that
help learners achieve competence.
They don't even consider providing
practice, guidance, or remediation—
things learners need, but may not
recognize they need when selecting
from a menu.

It's a Problem

We have much to learn from Web
design, but design practices effective
for the Web have also fostered many
e-learning applications that are
simply information retrieval services, not CCAF at all, and not very
effective. Designers must be wary.

Learning takes much more
than exposure to informa-
tion to succeed.

Application Design

Word processing, e-mail
managing, picture editing,
illustration drawing, tune
managing applications, and many
more types of software applications
set expectations for how one uses
a computer. We generally know
what to click, when we can type on
the keyboard, what we can touch,
how to delete, and so on. It's great
that e-learners arrive with many
skills for working with computers
already acquired. But e-learning is,
in some important ways, a unique
type of tool. Interface designs that
are appropriate for other types of
applications set standards that can
help e-learners feel at home. But
some of those standards can hamper
e-learning success. Learner interface
designers need to know the difference and choose carefully.

Learning Time

Frequently used software applications can take considerable time
to learn to use. This is acceptable
because of the many hours the tools
will be used. e-Learning applications

113

are often used for a short time—speed of learning and completion becomes a primary concern in many cases. And the learning of interest is not learning how to use the e-learning application, of course, but rather learning the content of the application.

The entire period of both learning to use an e-learning application and

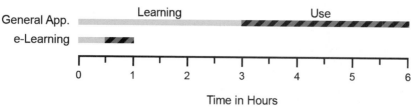

completing its use must often be a fraction of the time needed just to learn to use a general application. When designers follow the lead of general application design, they need to think whether they will be requiring learners to consume so much orientation time and effort that there will be insufficient time for learning and practicing the new skills taught in the e-learning. More intuitive mechanisms are often required.

Content-Unique Requirements

Unfortunately, the learner interface designer's task is sometimes complicated by the content of the courseware and the type of skills

being learned. These challenges must be met by using content-specific interface devices instead of the content-independent interfaces used by general applications.

Situation-Unique Requirements

When we are teaching the use of software applications, we find unique interface challenges. For example, buttons the application uses *NEXT, BACK, SAVE, QUIT* may be the same buttons the e-learning application is using. Learners have to differentiate which is which. Without good LID, learners can easily become confused.

It's a Problem

When interface protocols learned from the use of general software applications are appropriate, they can and should be used in e-learning applications to shorten the learning time and keep learner energy focused on learning the content and skills. But beyond the basic concepts and generic utilities (for example, Ctrl-p to print), general application models are often too general, too complicated, and too slow to acquire for short e-learning experiences.

Game Design

A wealth of useful interface design principles can be found in game design. Indeed, games are powerful teachers. What they teach isn't often very useful outside the bounds of the game itself, but games demonstrate how good interface can focus and maintain attention, how it can give powerful feedback, and how it can allow learners to practice, practice, practice.

Game designers (unlike many learner interface designers, ahem) know not to explain every nuance of an interface, especially at the beginning. In fact, game designers try to make discovery of interface capabilities a rewarding experience that occurs in the process of learning such things as procedures, systems, concepts, and facts (although they probably don't think in these terms). They actually demonstrate just-in-time training right within the microcosm of the game itself by helping learners acquire the ability to use new tools only when they have value. Players feel rewarded by learning the new things they can do, not burdened with trying to absorb too much at once.

But there are some cautions to consider in borrowing from game design for LID.

Time

One of the purposes of games is to retain interest over a significant amount of time. Instead of trying to minimize connect time, achieving the most learning in the shortest amount of time as we strive to do in e-learning, game designers try to lengthen the experience. The longer the entertainment time, the greater the product value is.

In e-learning, the longer the training takes, the more expensive it is. Consumption of learner time can be an enormous expense, to say nothing of lost productivity while in training, cost of training development, and so on. So while many game interface principles work for games because minimizing user time

115

is not an issue, there they are too slow for e-learning. We want the same level of psychological and emotional investment from our learners as games receive, of course, but we want it to happen in compressed time.

Expense

Because games are designed to attract very large, paying audiences, game design and development budgets are typically many multiples of what is available for designing and developing instructional applications. The exotic interface components, such as 3D controls and effects that game designers can create uniquely for each game and even each game level or sequence, are expensive and can require high-end programming to integrate into an application. Authoring tools are making more of these capabilities available at successively lower costs, but high-end interface features remain prohibitive for e-learning in many cases.

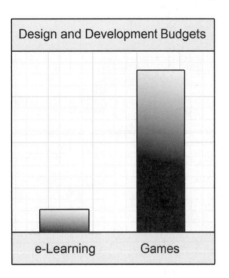

Design and Development Budgets

e-Learning   Games

Realism

It's important for some types of games to have a high level of realism—even, ironically, for fantasy games. Fascination can come simply from the novelty of the realism achieved. Once the novelty has worn off, the continuing value of the game is derived primarily from the cleverness of its strategy—the consequences of user actions.

In e-learning, the consequences of user actions are prime content—this is what well-designed applications offer learners. e-Learning designers make a mistake when they invest too much in visual realism or situational details that really don't matter. It can be hard to find the happy medium. There are those who value page-turning e-learning. At the other extreme are those who think high-fidelity simulations are always the best solution.

There are cases for high-fidelity simulation—when, for example, learners must attend to many simultaneous details, such as when flying an airplane or providing security surveillance. But in many cases, just a hint of reality can be enough to switch on the learner's imagination and create an excellent context for learning. Games really aren't about visual effects and animation, although these are valuable components. Games are about rules. Good rules, good game. Bad rules, bad game. Media just add or detract, reinforce or distract. The same applies to e-learning.

Hardware

The Wii game system wouldn't be able to provide the unique experiences it does without the great hardware engineered into it. The combination of unique gestures the system can sense along with the rapid processing of 3D graphics and multi-track sounds provides a wonderful platform. It can be tempting to try replicating some of these and other advanced interface inventions on systems having only generic input devices and general-purpose computation capabilities, but these attempts rarely succeed.

Fortunately, just as games are about rules, e-learning is about experiences—experiences that can often be created to perform well within the constraints of average personal computers. I've frequently criticized designs that obviously agonized more over button effects than over the impact of the interactions. It's easy to be sidetracked, but

very important to design well within the bounds of the hardware platform in use and to concentrate on what's really important.

Appropriateness

Just as great simulation fidelity is not always necessary, games aren't always appropriate or effective models for e-learning. Under the exciting prospect of building a game, it can be too easy to forge a game when it really wasn't justifiable. Sometimes fairly elaborate games are built for content that is relatively trivial to learn. Teaching simple content through a game can add time and unnecessary effort for both the developer and learner. And while games are often appreciated, they can also produce a bit of scorn when they obviously were built more to demonstrate the designer's or programmer's abilities than to improve the learning experience.

It's a Problem

Games offer an inexhaustible and still relatively untapped mine of inspiration and models for the learner interface designer. As long as we don't become caught in the trap of thinking that good e-learning can or should closely approximate an

Xbox game, we can learn important and valuable lessons from the ways video games solve interface problems. As always, it's imperative to keep focused on what has to be done to create a great learning experience, rather than creating interactive mechanisms that draw so much attention to themselves that they detract from CCAF.

8 | Doing the Right Things Versus Doing Things Right

Meaningful **Memorable**

3M Target

Motivational

With all the design details to be looked after, it's all too easy to get lost in details—about doing them right—and forget to provide a meaning, memorable, and motivational learning experience that produces useful behaviors.

It seems unfortunate to me that through decades of attempting to develop instruction based on the science of learning, it appears as though we've actually lost our way more often than found it. I don't disparage research on learning or instruction. I'm fascinated with such research, try to keep tabs on it, and look to it for potential design solutions. It's what people do with research findings that concerns me.

Because many variables entwine uniquely to determine a learner's perceptions, cognitive and physical behaviors, and learning outcomes, a large number of variables must be identified, controlled, and of the same value in the studies as in a project for applicability. This is almost *never* the case. And it's never the case that we have identical learners. So recommendations based on studies with necessarily different people in different situations are really educated guesses—informed guesses with some probable applicability—but guesses nonetheless. They are often bad recommendations for specific situations.

Science Versus Craft

We're on thin ice when we write instructional design guidebooks based more on research than on experience. It would be a challenge similar to writing a research-based guidebook on how to create a great movie (movies are far simpler things than e-learning in many ways). It could provide lists of things to consider. Considerations are helpful. It could note what has worked in specific instances and what has not. Also helpful. It could help readers understand how

Яapid readeR

- General user interface guidelines are important when not in conflict with learner interface design.

- Learner interface is a creative art respectful of both science and experience.

- The findings of human/computer interface research are often over-generalized.

directors have solved specific problems. Yes. But no one is expecting a science guidebook on moviemaking that would assure the creation of box office hits.

Thinking about movies a moment longer, a novel effect successful once often has far less appeal a second time. Novel techniques have a very short half-life. They lose their power with familiarity. Similarly, many interactive designs that were effective when interactive technologies were new have now lost their potency. User expectations affect perceptions and responses, and they are constantly changing. Moving targets are

particularly challenging for the slow process of scientific study.

So please don't suggest we've actually learned from research what connects with each of today's learners, stimulates their imaginations, motivates them to perform at higher levels, and produces better learning experiences. We're far from a generalized scientific know-how that guides us to deal well with the tremendous variability we face. Think of the magnitude of variables that are in play. Consider prior learner experience, age, goals, learning style, content relevance, skills, intelligences, interests, reading comprehension, listening skills, attention span, energy level, computer experience, and so on. There are definitely techniques and principles that help, and there are definitely people who have mastered the art of applying principles at the right times and places. But little of what we know to be effective has come into application because research studies have recommended it. Perhaps someday science will catch up. But today, we need more.

Guidelines Can Help

This chapter is a collection of guidelines culled from experience with many e-learning design and development projects—some successful, others, well, not as successful as hoped. We've learned a lot from both successful and unsuccessful designs. Because so many variables determine success, we have mostly guidelines only. We don't have a sound ability to generalize too broadly because the slightest variability can interfere with what would otherwise be a successful approach. Still, the items collected here seem to have broad applicability. They might claim the status of rules.

Some of these items are definitely user interface principles with broader applicability than the learner interface design principles of prime interest in all the other chapters of this book. But because they so often are abused, interfering with good learner interface design, I've included them here.

Feature-Rich e-Learning Creates Design Challenges

Page-turning applications are the simplest kinds of e-learning applications, yet they demonstrate how much design work is necessary to facilitate interactivity. Page-turners do what a book does—provide convenient access to pages of infor-

mation—although they tend to do it less well.

A page-turner interface would seem to be quite simple indeed. All that appears to be needed is a NEXT PAGE button and a PREVIOUS PAGE button. But this simple design becomes annoyingly restrictive if there are more than a few pages. For example, books make it easy to browse through pages very rapidly. We can jump to the end, back to the front, and so on. It provides comforting orientation.

So, for a page-turning interface, it might be helpful to also have a NEXT CHAPTER button and a PREVIOUS CHAPTER button. Of course, you'll probably want a QUIT button. What about a BOOKMARK PAGE button? Sounds good, but that might also require a "go to bookmark" button, which should probably be two buttons: GO TO PREVIOUS BOOKMARK and GO TO NEXT BOOKMARK. What about a way to remove a bookmark? ERASE BOOKMARK!

With a book, we also have quick access to the TABLE OF CONTENTS, the INDEX, possibly some APPENDICES, and information on the FRONT

COVER, BACK COVER. How about skipping through by looking for illustrations and tables? We often do that while inspecting books. More buttons for our page turner? We have already identified fifteen possible buttons! The figure at left shows only nine of the possible buttons on the interface, and it's already an overwhelming panel.

A "simple," button-based, page-turning interface competes poorly with a book for convenience.

This illustration is offered to underscore the point that interfaces are not easy to design, even when the operations they emulate are simple, such as reading a book. When the operations are numerous and sophisticated, as in feature-rich e-learning applications, the design challenges are very great indeed. They are often so insurmountable that highly beneficial features cannot be provided because no one can figure out a reasonable way for the learner to readily understand and control them.

Fortunately, our experience in building powerful interfaces is growing rapidly, technologies are advancing to give us a greater variety of recognizable learner gestures, and learners are increasingly familiar with computer interface conventions. But even the top software application designers still have difficulty designing interfaces we all can use without frustration. And no matter how many interfaces one has created, almost everyone underestimates the effort required to come up with a good design.

As an e-learning application takes shape, the simple learner interface design originally conceived can begin to sag under the weight of incremental features. As we've seen, a large count of options, each of which might be clear and easy enough to use, can make an interface onerous. I have attended plenty of design meetings during which useful features were abandoned simply because the number of features had become overwhelming.

Miscellaneous Guidelines

To help, the following is an unordered list of miscellaneous design principles to consider. Many fall into the category of user interface design principles rather than uniquely learner interface design (LID) principles and are therefore not covered in-depth elsewhere in this book, but they impinge on LID and are therefore important to consider.

M1. Differentiate Active and Inactive Elements

It seems obvious, manifest, inviolable. One should not (1) run over pedestrians, (2) put poisons on the spice rack, or (3) make active and inactive screen elements look alike.

This clearly has to be said, although I don't understand why. Designers frequently make this obvious and grievous error—to the frustration of every user. Many Web sites, for example, whether instructional or not, underline some inactive headings just to set them off. The underlining makes them look like hypertext links. Bad! Sometimes there is even underlined hypertext in close proximity. How confusing this is!

Apple generally has brilliant user interface design in all their products, but sometimes even they blunder. Take, for example, the insanely successful iTunes application. I could not figure out how to set the name of my new phone. Online help didn't. But an Internet search revealed that you can double-click in the selection menu to change the name. There's no format indication of this capability, no "invitation" to click.

Look to the right where information about the phone is presented. You cannot click the name field to change it, although this gesture seems quite plausible. But did you know that, while you can't click the name field or the following two items (capacity and version), the following two fields, formatted identically to those above, respond to clicks? Amazing inconsistency and obscurity. Don't follow this model.

M2. Stay Put

Good screen design is difficult. No doubt about it. Each screen layout presents unique challenges, but you can move things around a bit to accommodate the specific contents of each page. Different background, border, or font colors might look better with different content elements. It's easy to make these changes with today's software. *But don't!* Stick with one or just a small number of basic screen layouts, carrying them forward from one interactive instance to another. The framework will become a recognized context that helps learners understand which rules of engagement are in effect without having to continually reassess the situation. Consistency helps learners notice exactly what has changed and thus should not be overlooked. If everything has changed in appearance, learners must assess everything to see what has changed in substance.

M3. Avoid Erasing the Screen

Positive screen inertia is pretty much destroyed when the screen is completely erased. Our confidence that we know what is and is not in

the space becomes uncertain. Even if what appears after the erasure seems just like the screen on display a second ago, we instinctively and appropriately begin a search to see whether anything changed. If anything has changed, every future screen erasure is also a signal to learners that they should carefully review the entire layout before going on, wasting precious attention span.

M4. Use Interface Conventions Consistently

This is yet another common practice that shouldn't have to be mentioned. Mixing conventions seems so obviously detrimental. But it occurs with alarming frequency.

Apple Computer is known for the excellence of their interface designs. When they introduced the Macintosh computer, they provided a carefully delineated set of user interface rules for software developers. The rules promoted strong consistency among applications, such as having a FILE menu at the top left corner of the screen followed by an EDIT menu, and so on. Many of these conventions continue today, even on other operating systems, because of the logic of the arrangement and the advantages of consistency—most notably, the ease of use.

M5. Don't Crowd the Screen

White space is important. When designers refer to white space, they actually mean the empty space used to separate items and to help draw attention to important elements. White space doesn't have to be white, although white and black are often good color choices for open space. It can be any color—even a subtle gradient or pattern. The background should contrast strongly with other display elements and allow the eye to focus comfortably on display elements without distraction.

M6. Present Text Effectively

Remember always, people don't like reading text on the screen and, what they do read, they read with reduced comprehension. Learners generally want and expect action-based encounters when using a computer.

Eyes glaze over when they see large blocks of text, and learners are likely to exercise every option you give them to skip over it.

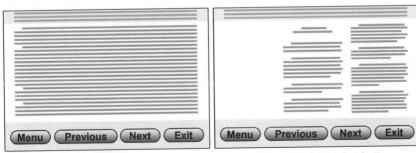

If text absolutely, positively has to be on the screen, use
short lines and no more than five lines per block.

If you can't use audio or otherwise omit on-screen text, use short lines and blocks. Try not to use columns wider than forty characters for monotype fonts, fifty characters with variable spacing. Don't justify the right margin (for left-to-right text, vice versa for right-to-left). A ragged margin helps align the eye. It's best to leave a blank line after every five lines, although allowing up to seven-line blocks may be acceptable, especially if shorter blocks surround them.

Make judicious use of scrolling text. Scrolling text has advantages for designers. With scrolling text, designers can use as much or as little space for the text as is convenient for their screen design. The learner then scrolls the text within the established boundaries.

Unfortunately, scrolling text has some disadvantages for learners. For example, learners are sometimes allowed to see too few lines at a time, making it hard to maintain context. Depending on where scrolling happens to stop, text may divide at awkward points, requiring learners to jostle everything around with all the attendant distraction. As text scrolls, readers often have a hard time focusing on their current positions. After scrolling, they may have to begin reading at a somewhat random point to see whether they have scrolled too much, not enough, or as far as they actually intended. Rescanning is disruptive, tiring, and bothersome. It can definitely sap the learner's motivation.

If you can keep the amount of text to a minimum, you may be able to avoid scrolling text altogether. That's often best.

M7. Use a Small Color Palette Purposefully

There are lots of colors to choose from. Hundreds, thousands, millions. The more the better, right? No. Almost the reverse.

Color has learning value only when it (1) systematically highlights, groups, or classifies selected objects (that is, the color has meaning), (2) creates helpful realism, or (3) enhances focus, clarity, and legibility. Displaying many colors at one time makes none of them valuable; they just fight with each other for attention, with none winning. Too many colors: none of them have much impact. Inconsistent use of color: noisy, confused message. No meaningful use of color: missed opportunity.

M8. Use a Small Number of Fonts Purposefully

Oh, please. Don't use a plethora of fonts just because they're there, because you like each one of them, because it's possible, or for any other reason. We are not writing ransom notes or creating walls of graffiti. A jumble of fonts makes reading screen text even more difficult and unpleasant than it normally is. Severely restrict the number of fonts you use. Just as with the application of colors, change fonts only when there is a clear reason to do so. Define your rules for usage and stick with them.

You'll find some helpful guidelines in these resources: Robin Williams and John Tollet, *The Non-Designer's Web Book*; Kevin Mullet and Darrell Sano, *Designing Visual Interfaces*.

Two fonts may well enhance the look and readability of your content. You are likely to be safe selecting one font that has serifs—those fine little lines at the end of strokes on characters like those found in the Times New Roman font. The other font should not have serifs. The ubiquitous Arial and Helvetica fonts are called "sans serif" because they have no serifs.

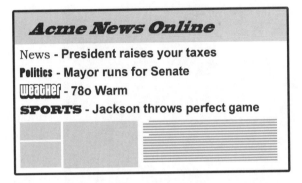

"Ransom note" typography makes reading screen text very difficult.

Serif and sans serif typefaces

M9. Go on an Eye Candy Diet

Yet another type of distraction that happens primarily, I suppose, because it has become possible, is extravagant visual adornment.

Glitz. Eye candy. Pretty. Fun. But, like chocolate cara-mel ice cream sundaes, it's bad for you.

It's hard enough to accurately convey messages of any complexity, let alone do so while nearby icons flaunt "isn't-this-cool" acrobatics. The learner receives mixed messages. *Don't look at the button pulsing with readiness to jump you somewhere else. Don't look at the header that's begging to show you what other things you could be doing. No, concentrate on the static stuff, because that's where your attention should be for now. We put those ornaments here just to make your experience more pleas-ant. Please ignore them!*

Glitz is usually there because someone wanted to show off his ability to create it, because everything else he was doing was boring, or because he didn't know how to create sound learning experiences.

Glitzy screens contribute nothing to learning.

Glitz has appeal, even to those serious about obtaining a good return from their e-learning invest-ment. But if resources are diverted to ornamentation instead of to quality interactions, the payoff in perfor-mance outcomes is not going to be what it could be.

M10. Feature Learning Activities, Not Navigation

Navigation capabilities are impor-tant for most learning applications, but they are in many ways like a picture frame. They need to be supportive but not in competition

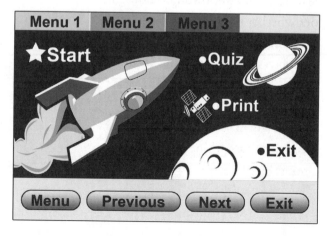

for the viewer's attention. Some navigation systems are distracting simply because of the strength of their graphic design. It is often easy to justify the extra time and effort to embellish navigation components because they are used repeatedly throughout an application. But the resulting visual refinement of navigation elements can draw attention away from the sometimes plain appearance of content.

Much worse, however, is when the navigation forces learners through bewildering contortions, consuming much too much thought. This can happen when developers try to develop a generalized navigation interface and use it everywhere, even when it's far more than what's needed or helpful. With some complex navigations, learners just give up and use the most essential features. They get through, but wonder whether they missed things they shouldn't have and whether there was an easier way to get through.

M11. Maintain Focus

Ever look at a screen and wonder which of all the things there you should be attending to? It happens when the visual space is unfamiliar or loaded with complexity. With all the interactive and informative elements we can provide simultaneously, it becomes all too easy to overwhelm learners. Valuable techniques that help learners focus on the right things include spatial placement, grouping, animation, and contrast.

M12. Keep Navigation in Its Place

Two seemingly opposite approaches help differentiate navigation from content and keep focus on the content: fixed screen divisions and floating navigation panels.

Fixed divisions. Anchoring navigation into a space continuously reserved for it is often best. Once learners become accustomed to the navigation structures, they develop an ability to see past them and ignore them almost completely except when they need to select a feature. It's what psychologists call accommodation, and it occurs when a stimulus becomes so familiar that it no longer draws our attention. Animation and sound effects can override accommodation

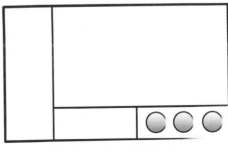

Anchored navigation

and bring special attention to navigation components when needed. Otherwise, the navigation sits quietly; it's helpful but transparent.

Floating panels. Sometimes the entire screen is needed for content components, such as when simulating a software application or operating system that normally commands the whole screen. In this situation, layering the screen can provide both screen division and the ability to see all areas. The navigation panel should be designed to contrast with but not upstage information displays. It should be easy to move, because the learner may have to take an active role in moving the panel out of the way if the software can't find a reliable basis for doing it automatically.

M13. Group Visual Elements

There is a tendency to put too much information on the screen at one time. Indeed, even with today's high-resolution color displays, it's a challenge to effectively present as much information as can be done well on a printed page. It is very easy to overload or dazzle the learner with too many displayed content items, interactivity options, and navigation controls. Still, context is important, and dispensing with it isn't a good solution to a clutter problem. It obviously wouldn't do to present a graphic on one screen followed by its description on the next and questions about it on the next. Interactivity designers are constantly grappling with the need to make the most effective use of the space.

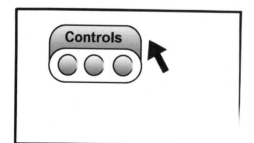
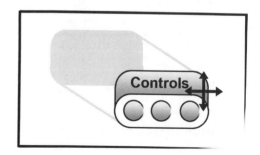

A floating navigation panel can be moved by the learner as needed.

Grouping is a good way to reduce the perception of clutter and to increase the amount of information that can be displayed. Leaving blank space between groups of items helps to set them off and draws the eye to them more effectively.

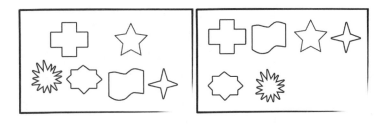

Grouping, as in the right figure, makes it easy to see all the content.

Text headings gain utility from good spacing and grouping. They should often be much larger than the body of text they label to establish hierarchy and to break up the monotony of text walls. But their relationship to text and the hierarchical structuring breaks down as the distance between them and the text increases. It's important to keep headings closely grouped with their respective text to keep the eye from wandering. The benefits are double: the relationship is strengthened and space is released.

Note that all of the items in the left column appear also in the right column, but see how much easier it is to read the right column and to assimilate the organization.

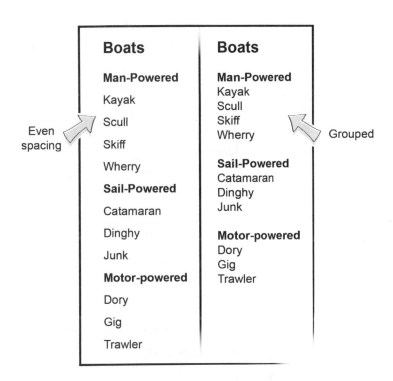

Text headings gain power when spaced and grouped.

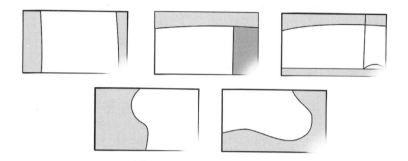

Asymmetrical divisions help define spaces and provide identity.

In dividing display space, it's almost always best to use asymmetrical divisions, which are more comfortable to view and more effective in communicating with learners than are symmetrical designs. Contrasting proportions also help define spaces and give them functional identity.

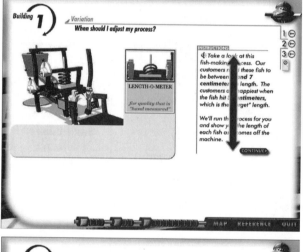

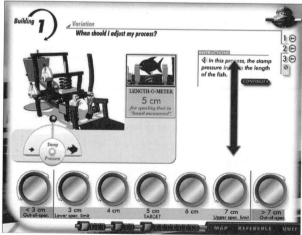

In the screenshots shown here the text is animated to help learners focus attention there.

M14. Animate for a Purpose

Just as unique or out-of-place things draw our attention, we are also predisposed to look at moving objects. Content can be animated in attention-getting ways that really help draw our attention.

In a large-scale project developed by DaimlerChrysler's Quality Institute to teach statistical process control, screens needed to display a variety of large charts, graphs, and tables. Instructive text had to be worked in and around the displays that dominated the screen. It would be easy for learners not to see important information among all the displayed elements.

A unique, animated technique was used to present new text. Each time text appeared on the screen, it smoothly dropped down as if on a window blind. The animation drew the learners' visual attention to the area.

Animation has a downside. It's fleeting. While an animated process can show time-related effects, it can also be difficult to recognize and assess actions as they flash by. Slowing processes helps. So does providing a slider so that learners can control the speed, pause, and even watch the action in reverse. But many times the expense of animation isn't needed. A series of still frames, while perhaps not as cool, can actually communicate better.

M15. Use Contrast to Communicate More Clearly

Contrast exists in size, position, texture, scale, animation, volume, timbre, saturation, transparency, and color. In general, our attention is drawn to things that are different—that contrast with others.

A good rule for contrast, whether it's color, text size, or any other parameter: If two items aren't the same, make sure learners can easily discern the difference. Subtle differences can be attractive, but they often confuse functionality. So make contrasts big and bold.

M16. Make Text Legible

Why wouldn't you? Don't know. But so often I see text that's very hard to read. Be alert for illegible text. Some examples:

➢ Red text on a blue background (or vice versa) doesn't work. Your eye can't focus well on these two colors simultaneously.

➢ Not all learners will have great vision, so keep text larger than necessary for people with average vision.

➢ Don't put small or lightweight text over photos or illustrations that have varied colors or textures. It can be impossible to read and looks bad.

M17. Sound Off

Sounds add a strong dimension to interactive applications. Just as with color and animation, however, sounds have as much ability to be distracting and annoying as they do to be helpful and pleasing.

Sound effects can be valuable design assets when they:

Convey information, such as:

➢ The learner's gesture has been recognized.

➢ An option or process is being applied.

➢ An effective solution or correct answer has been entered.

➢ A significant goal has been reached.

➢ A selected option is not applicable.

➢ A value is out of range.

➢ The maximum or minimum value has been set.

➢ Time is running out.

Support learner focus:

➢ Sound effects should usually be very short in duration—only long enough to be distinctive.

➢ Sounds should be pleasant (even for most errors).

➢ Sounds should not broadcast failures to nearby persons, as it can be quite defocusing to all. The public announcement of successes can even be disturbing, although probably less harmful.

➢ Amuse learners.

➢ Convey an energetic, light-hearted attitude.

➢ Help learners realize that mistakes can be instructive.

Although there's something appealing about sounds, perhaps just because of their novelty (an attribute that fades quickly with repetition), it's easy to use sounds in ways that

detract from learning. Designers need to use much care.

Don't:

➢ Make noise without much reason.

➢ Confuse learners with inconsistent use of sounds.

➢ Let sounds play too late or out of synchronization.

➢ Irritate learners by. . .
  ➢ Playing sounds repeatedly.
  ➢ Assaulting the ear.
  ➢ Playing sounds for extended periods.
  ➢ Embarrassing learners.

M18. Invite Gestures—Static Invitations

You can simplify mouse-driven interactions by highlighting click and rollover-sensitive objects or distinguishing them in some other consistent manner (color or grouping, for example), thereby inviting learners to consider using these interactive objects and informing them of the gestures that will be recognized. We should use different indications for click, rollover, or drag activation or any other activating gesture. Invitations might take the form of a surrounding glow, a drop shadow, a bright color, underlining, 3D perspective, alignment in a banner, and so on, as long as the use is consistent. Using standards found frequently in other applications or the Internet reduces learning time and trial-and-error mistakes.

Highlights should always appear when an object is active and never when it's not. Of course, the same style of highlighting should never be applied to static objects.

M19. Invite Gestures—Dynamic Invitations

The message that an object is active should be confirmed by, for example, a highlight that appears when the mouse pointer rolls over the object. Rollovers need only indicate that they have been activated with the pointer over them, whereas click, double-click, and drag gestures may need to be invited with a second-level invitation such as a change in the pointer's shape.

It is also good practice to let users know when things they might expect to be active are not. "Dimmed" buttons are a good example. When a button appears darkened, grayed, or colorless in contrast to its usual state, users can understand that the button is inactive. A common mistake in current design styles is failing to distinguish inactive from deselected states.

M20. Rollover and Play Alive

There is something pleasing about making something happen simply by moving the pointer over an object. Nearly effortless retrieval of helpful information can be an excellent aid for thinking and an outstanding capability of e-learning. But rollovers aren't universally applicable. Designers need to be careful with them.

Don't use rollovers when:

1. The action they initiate is destructive, time-consuming, or difficult to undo. Rollovers are easily tripped by a haphazard mouse movement.

2. The object is also programmed to respond to a click or double-click. Learners may never realize two or more levels of service are available.

3. The response to a rollover blocks access to adjacent rollovers. Learners may have trouble triggering the rollover they want because other pop-ups block the path.

4. Responses to rollovers are slow. Rollovers demand quick responses and exits to be satisfactory, mainly because of the risk of unintentionally triggering one, interrupting thought and flow.

135

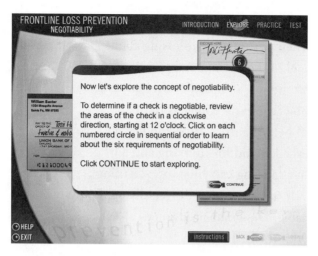

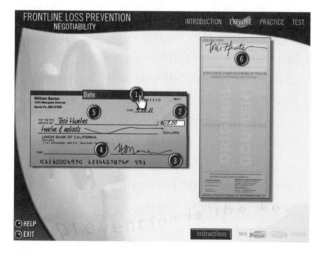

In this program, the user learns to verify the six components of a check that must be valid in order for the check to be negotiable. As the user rolls over each of the six components with the mouse, the verification sequence number pulses and displays the name of that item.

Some rollover "do's":

1. Make sure the response to a rollover is nondestructive.

2. Make sure that, on rollout, the screen is left as it was previous to the rollover.

3. Make sure it's clear which object triggered the current rollover action.

4. Keep response information short and much of the underlying screen visible.

Clicking. Pointing to an object is one level of skill. Clicking an object isn't much more difficult (although knowing that you need to click an object can be another matter, as previously described). But double-clicking is surprisingly difficult for many learners.

M21. Double Your Clicks; Double Your Frustration

Clicking an object to select it becomes very natural for frequent computer users, but for some, clicking an object takes a bit of mental adjustment and fortitude, especially when a click sometimes initiates action and other times harmlessly selects an object for future action. It's extremely important for applications to respond consistently to every click. If one item opens with a single click, but other items open only with a double-click, significant confusion and anxiety can build. Truly, one little design slip and learners feel they can't trust your interface.

In response to some learner-interface designs tested in an evaluation lab I ran at Control Data, complete with one-way mirrors and a sound-proof observation room into which we sequestered reluctant designers, a frequent devastating comment heard from users was, "I feel so stupid. I can't figure out what I'm supposed to do." It takes very, very little inconsistency for learners to feel lost and frustrated.

It's surprising how obscure double-click interfaces can be, let alone right-button clicks. The problem is generally that there's no signal to say "single-click for this function and double-click for this other one." When used, double-clicking should be a shortcut for functions that can be requested in other ways. It's also probably best to stick to using double clicks as an "open" command and nothing else.

Three general suggestions with respect to double-clicking:

1. Avoid it.
2. If it's really necessary, use it often enough that learners both get the hang of it and reap enough benefit from the shortcut.
3. Develop separate, distinguishable, rollover invitations for single and double clicks.

M22. Minimize Drag-and-Drop Woes

If double-clicking is an obstacle for learners, drag-and-drop gestures can be almost impossible for them. It's unfortunate, because there are times when this gesture seems very appropriate for the skill being taught.

Some considerations:

1. Drag-and-drop interactions are often used when they're quite unnecessary. Using a more complex set of user gestures, as drag-and-drop interactions require, doesn't automatically increase instructional interactivity. Carefully consider your alternatives. (See alternative forms of essentially the same question, each using a different interaction interface in Michael Allen's *Guide to e-Learning*, pages 281 to 283. The drag-and-drop interaction is hardest for learners to perform, yet often yields the same information about the learner's knowledge as do simpler interactions.)

2. To make drag-and-drop as learner-friendly as possible, provide cues before, during, and after the interaction:

➤ **Clearly identify movable objects and target areas.** For example, movable objects (and only movable objects) might have drop shadows, and target areas might have distinguishing borders.

➤ **Invite dragging.** On rolling over a movable object, change the pointer shape to confirm that the object can

be moved. For example, the arrow pointer could change to a hand shape when it is over a movable object, and the hand could close as if grasping the object while the mouse button is depressed.

➤ **Invite target consideration.** When an object is being dragged, target areas can take on additional highlighting, such as a glow.

➤ **Confirm proximity.** Indicate what dropping the object at the current position will mean. For example, if it's close enough to one of several alternative targets, highlight the one that would respond to the drop. Such confirmation will help minimize mistakes and the need for subsequent correction.

You can see how carefully instructional drag-and-drop interfaces must be devised. Designers will always find their interactions to be far more intuitive than learners will. Because of the inherent risks, avoid drag-and-drop when it has no genuine advantage over other gestures. If you must use drag-and-drop gestures for instructional operations, take extra care to provide sufficient assistance and feedback.

M23. Consider Click-to-Place Instead of Drag-and-Drop

A simpler interface that can often substitute for drag-and-drop interactions is click-to-place. The learner first clicks an object to be placed. The object highlights. The learner then clicks a desired location and the object is animated into the clicked location. No dragging or complex highlighting is involved.

If identification of objects to be moved is not a critical part of the interaction, items to be moved can be identified for the learner one at a time. In this case, learners need only identify desired locations. It's faster and simpler yet.

Procedural Guidelines

Finally, a note about process. Research, tradition, and experience are all guides to be respected and considered, but reality is final truth. To succeed, one needs to be

pragmatic and objective. We seek the shortest path to a test of our best hunches. Did we really get it right?

As we've discussed at great length in the other two library series books, an iterative approach is the only sane approach. Linear approaches always pass up opportunities and fail because of a faulty assumption here and there. So how can you be assured that, within your time, budget, and available skills, you can succeed? Perhaps your best assurance is in the process you choose.

Here are three really important tips to keep in mind as you design your successful learner interface:

M24. Don't Start from Scratch

There are two layers of navigation and interface features that are almost always required in e-learning applications. The top layer includes features for topic selection, overview access, progress recall, quit, and resume. Context- and content-specific features provide the second layer, including support for entering and editing responses, controlling simulations, and accessing related resource information and help. Experienced designers know how to handle these structures and rarely start completely from scratch. It is

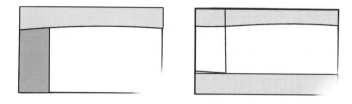

quite effective and expeditious to adapt previous designs that have proven successful and flexible.

If you are starting from scratch, reserve screen display areas. It can be difficult to know what screen divisions are going to work best at the start of a new project unless content elements and their requirements are known in specific detail. For this reason, it's often best in the initial prototypes to divide display real estate as follows:

➤ A standardized heading area that might also show progress and/or current position within the application

➤ One large primary area, perhaps taking about half the screen

➤ One smaller secondary area that is itself significantly larger than any remaining spaces

➤ An area reserved for instructions

➤ Area(s) reserved for prompts, alerts, helps, scoring, and other miscellaneous items

➤ An area reserved for navigation

As prototypes evolve, the appropriate numbers and sizes of reserved spaces will become clear. It's very easy to underestimate space requirements. If you're not careful with space allocations early on, it becomes necessary to sacrifice consistency. With the pressure on, screens become overfull, disorganized, and unlike anything originally intended.

M25. Let Others Judge

There are, in fact, many learner interface design solutions known to experienced design teams, but even experts do some pretty horrendous things. Interface designers rarely have much trouble using their own interfaces, so they often conclude too easily that their designs are intuitive and user-friendly for everyone. Thankfully, it doesn't really take an expert to judge whether an interface is easy to use. It does, however, take some objective evaluation and some open-mindedness.

Theory and experience are helpful, but the acid test is how effective a design is when used by learners. It is important to watch others use interface designs without comment or guidance. Don't just ask testers what they think; watch them.

Through observation, you may find learners who overlook simple ways to do things or avoid using options they really need to use. Learners don't always realize what they don't realize.

M26. Plan for More

Experienced designers know that more controls and interface features than initially expected will be desired and probably added. In their prototypes, they are careful to both reserve space and to delay refinement of global interface protocols until the desired learning experiences have taken clear shape.

Summary

An overall synthesis of the various learner options is essential to bring unity to the design, set learner expectations, fulfill those expectations, minimize the learning effort, promote use of valuable learning aids, and prevent unnecessary learner mistakes. Consistency in the application's features and compliance with established protocols found in contemporary software are also crucial. Added features may require you to rethink the initial design, so don't lock things in too soon. Again, leave space and, even more importantly, also reserve some time to rework your design once your tests with some learners confirm what works and what doesn't.

While the bulk of the design work of e-learning must naturally be devoted to devising meaningful and memorable learning experiences, it's a mistake to spend all the design time on content, necessarily making short shrift of the interface. The interface design affects the quality and effectiveness of every interaction. In many ways, it determines the effectiveness of e-learning applications. Getting it right is not just nice, it's critical.

Part Four

Examples

9 | Examples

While no example could apply and demonstrate all of the learner interface guidelines put forth in the previous chapters, it's probably equally true that no example demonstrates the application of only a single guideline. Example applications are therefore mixtures of guidelines woven into a solution. The following examples are all taken from e-learning applications designed and built within real-world constraints because all of them are real applications, many of which are in use today.

You'll note that in every case, the design is built on a strong context, as is the hallmark of excellent design. Many interactions tend to occur on a single "page."

Example 1.
Corrective Lenses—Optics

Tessa can see close objects better than far objects. This means that she is near-sighted or myopic. In this activity, you will use what you've just learned in the exercise about sphere power values and move the slider right or left to calculate the correct sphere power value for Tessa.

Principles Applied
CONNECT

Learners will take various roles in the production of corrective eye lenses, but all will find it valuable to understand the basic principles. The designer created a strong, humanized context, that of writing an accurate

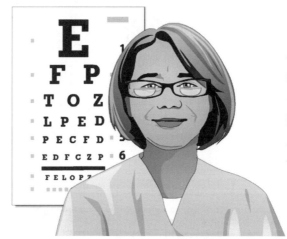

Screen capture courtesy of Essilor of America, Inc.

For each example, applicable guidelines from previous chapters are referenced by number and listed. A downloadable reference guide of all the guidelines is available through the Allen Interactions Web site, http://info.alleninterac-tions.com/e-learning-interface-reference-guide

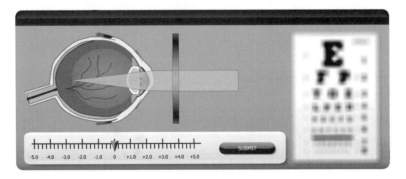

Starting position

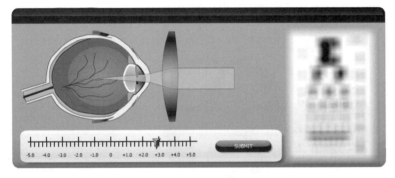

Adjusted in the wrong direction

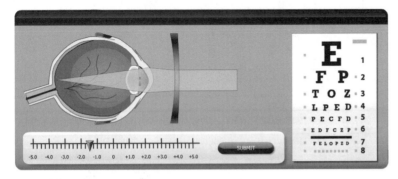

Perfect adjustment

prescription for Tessa's corrective lenses, even though learners at this point are still in the process of learning basic concepts and skills, such as distinguishing nearsightedness (myopia) from farsightedness (hyperopia).

C1. Demonstrate that you know your learners. (b)

C2. Select meaningful and beneficial challenges. (a)

C3. Activities should relate to what learners do now and will do after skill development. (b)

C5. Use theatrical devices. (d)

C7. Keep the story going. (b)

C8. The story continues. (a, b)

C12. Don't skip over the practicalities. (b)

C13. Consequences, judgments, explanations—of these, the greatest is consequences. (a)

EMPOWER

The learner immediately takes an active and personal role, rather than attempting to learn key concepts and terms theoretically without context or any personal stake. Learners simply and directly move the slider left and right to achieve the objective, observing multiple, interrelated effects simultaneously. Easy control, easy interaction, easy learning.

E2. Maintain space and place. (a, b, c, d)

E3. Make learning easier by eliminating distractions. (a)

E4. Present the challenge in context. (b)

E5. Differentiate controls from displays. (a)

E8. Build response opportunities into the context. (a, b)

ORCHESTRATE

The designer demonstrates interconnections of concepts, causes and effects, and does so simply and clearly for learners. Curvature of the lens changes, image convergence focuses at different points within the eye, and the clarity of the eye chart changes. Feedback is continuous and visual.

O2. Think role playing. (a, b)

O3. Provide realistic distractions and confusion. (a, b)

O5. Stay in character. (a)

O6. Make a good first impression. (a, b)

O7. Pop the challenge. (a)

O15. Prefer controls to inputs. (a)

O16. Match controls to learner readiness. (b)

Example 2. Infant/Toddler Safety Hazards

It's 7:30 a.m. Children are in your daycare center. Are you aware of your safety hazards?

In this activity, you will examine typical infant/toddler areas to identify potential safety hazards. Check indoor and outdoor environments. Use your observation skills and your knowledge of infants and toddlers to identify things that might be unsafe.

Screen captures courtesy of Teaching Strategies, Inc.

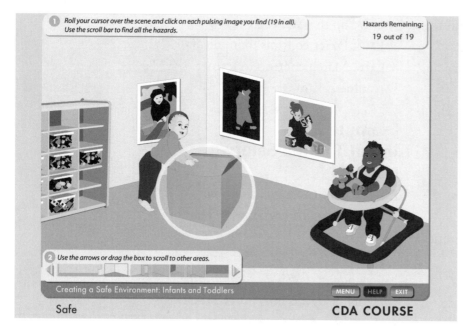

There are nineteen safety hazards in the scene. Can you find them all?

The learner uses the navigation bar at the lower left to scan from area to area, from room to room and even outside. The learner is looking for nineteen hazardous situations, as indicated at the upper right.

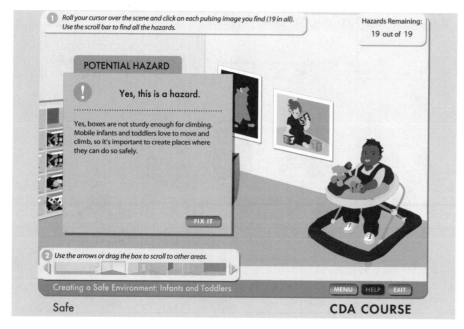

When an unsafe situation is spotted and the learner rolls the mouse pointer over it, a white circular highlight appears to invite action (a mouse click, in this case).

Feedback is provided along with a button to "fix it."

A safe alternative replaces the original hazard, and the target count reduces.

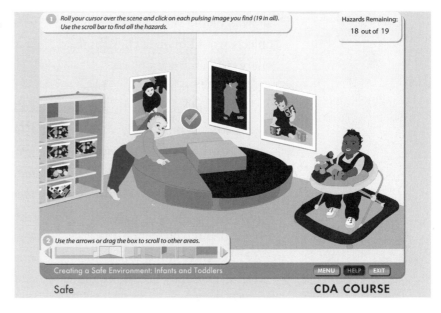

Principles Applied
CONNECT
Safety of children put in the care of others creates concern. Visualizing the environment builds on this concern and creates an energized learning environment.

C1. Demonstrate that you know your learners. (a, b)

C5. Use theatrical devices. (d)

C6. Nest dramatic human consequences in the challenge. (a)

C7. Keep the story going. (b)

C9. Context is almost everything. Choose wisely. (c)

C12. Don't skip over practicalities. (b)

EMPOWER
The designer provided an easy way for learners to navigate through a large visual display while maintaining controls in a comfortable, fixed space. Very little computer use dexterity is required for learners to explore spaces and identify concerns.

E1. Be visual. (a)

E2. Maintain space and place. (a)

E4. Present the challenge in context. (a, b)

E5. Differentiate controls from displays. (d)

E6. Use contextual elements to compose feedback. (a)

E8. Build response opportunities into the context. (a)

E10. Make challenge identification part of an action-orientated task. (a)

ORCHESTRATE
The learner can scan rooms and spaces, identifying problems in any order. Consequences of not identifying a problem are discussed when a problem is identified. A stronger design orchestration might have allowed all objects to be clickable, with only a fixed number of errors

allowed before starting over. All objects would invite a click, both safety risks and safe objects.

O2. Think role playing. (b)

O3. Provide realistic distractions and confusion. (a)

O4. Compare performance to objectives. (a)

O6. Make a good first impression. (b)

O7. Pop the challenge. (a)

O12. Create conditions—the "if"—gradually becoming more subtle from one exercise to the next. (a)

O13. To set up challenges, familiarize learners with the conditions,

actions, and consequences individually. (a)

O15. Prefer controls to inputs. (a)

Example 3. Police Officer Training I

We have evidence that gang activity may be involved, so we need to identify their whereabouts and activities as quickly as possible. We're dispatching cars to determine whether there is evidence of gang activity. You take this one. Give us an accurate report of activity in your assigned area ASAP.

This example has similarity to the LID used above for daycare center risk identification, but deals with

Screen captures courtesy of Commission on Peace Officer Standards and Training

very different content. It also adds speed as a criterion, simulating scanning from a moving car. Learners "drive" a car (as shown via a scrolling background viewed through a car window), spot indicators of gang activity, and report key details.

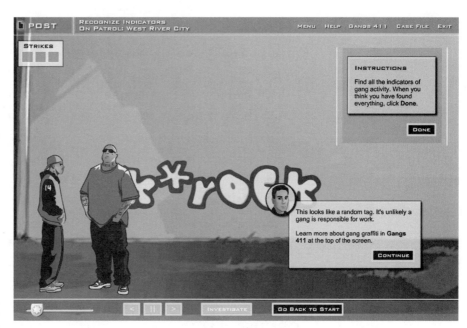

Learners then need to approach suspicious scenes and note the indicators they feel are significant (by clicking them). A lead officer and mentor pops up to provide feedback on the learner's choices.

Principles Applied
CONNECT

Police officer trainees are put into the context of identifying signs specific to gang activity as opposed to simple graffiti, group activities, and non-gang misconduct. The challenge is inherently interesting to trainees and either allows them to demonstrate their proficiency or develop it as needed.

C1. Demonstrate that you know your learners. (a, b)

C3. Activities should relate to what learners do now and will do after skill development. (a, b)

C5. Use theatrical devices. (d)

C7. Keep the story going. (a)

C12. Don't skip over practicalities. (a)

EMPOWER

The motion slider and buttons allow backing up, but these are artificial controls that can be withheld when learners have advanced or are being tested.

E2. Maintain space and place. (a, b, c, d)

E3. Make learning easier by eliminating distractions. (a)

E4. Present the challenge in context. (b)

E5. Differentiate controls from displays. (c)

E7. If the feedback isn't intrinsic, create a unique visual identity for it. (a)

E8. Build response opportunities into the context. (a)

E10. Make challenge identification part of an action-orientated task. (a)

E11. Empower learners with meaningful control. (b)

E12. Make control comforting and convenient. (b)

E14. Make states clear. (b)

ORCHESTRATE

The LID here is fascinating, as time and motion are critical aspects of the context. Images slide by in "play mode" to replicate the experience of looking out the window of a moving police car. Feedback is provided as mentorship from an advisor.

O1. Think theater. Think experience. Be dramatic. (a)

O2. Think role playing. (a)

O3. Provide realistic distractions and confusion. (a, b)

O6. Make a good first impression. (a, b)

O7. Pop the challenge. (a)

O8. Instill a sense of confidence. (a)

O12. Create conditions—the "if"—gradually becoming more subtle from one exercise to the next. (c)

O13. To set up challenges, familiarize learners with the conditions, actions, and consequences individually. (a)

O15. Prefer controls to inputs. (a, b)

O16. Match controls to content. (a)

Example 4. Police Officer Training II

In this example we continue our work with gang awareness training. Remember, approach suspicious situations carefully and with respect. Don't fail to fill out your Field Interview (FI) cards during each contact with suspects.

In the first step of training created for these skills, learners engage in a field interview with suspected gang members and must use the right questioning approach, exactly as they need to do in the real world.

Feedback is provided through changes in graphics (demeanor of suspects), replies, thought bubbles, and comments from a mentor.

Then, in follow-up to the conversation, the learner must enter a description as he or she would write on an FI card. The key is to provide the right level of detail.

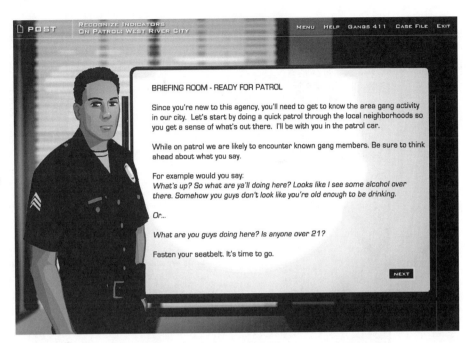

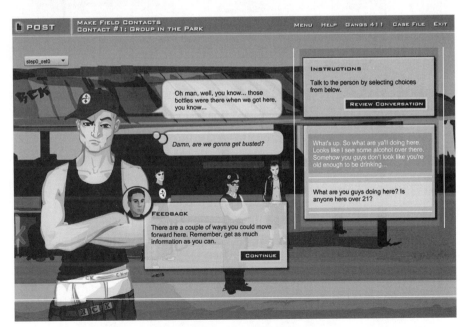

Screen captures courtesy of Commission on Peace Officer Standards and Training

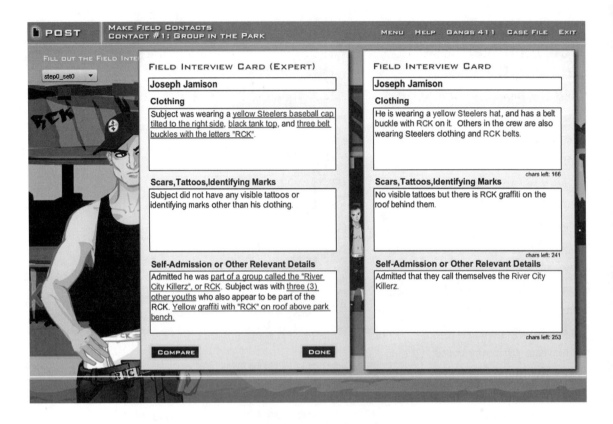

Remarkable, fascinating, and very useful feedback is given through a computerized comparison of the learner's notes with what the expert would have written. Key items recognized in the learner's FI are highlighted as they are in the expert's FI card.

Principles Applied
CONNECT

Trainees are put in situations that project obvious tension and potentially extreme risks. This connects with people.

C1. Meeting of minds. (a)

C2. Select meaningful and beneficial challenges. (a, b)

C3. Activities should relate to what learners do now and will do after skill development. (a, b)

C4. It's not just what you say, but how you say it. (a)

C5. Use theatrical devices. (a, b, d)

C7. Keep the story going. (a, b)

C12. Don't skip over practicalities. (a)

EMPOWER

Learners select from questions to ask and freely construct reports on their field interviews. While selection of questions is certainly different from constructing a conversation, officers learn important principles of what to say and what not to say from this interaction. Selection is both more realistic to author and easier for learners. However, within the defined framework of a conducted interview, it was possible for the authors and developers to provide learners very effective practice on constructing their reports.

E2. Maintain space and place. (a)

E4. Present the challenge in context. (a, b)

E6. Use contextual elements to compose feedback. (a)

E10. Make challenge identification part of an action-orientated task. (a)

E11. Empower learners with meaningful control. (a)

ORCHESTRATE

Although evaluating open-ended text or spoken responses is difficult, technology continues to advance. This example demonstrates that even within the constraints of common project budgets and resources, when learner-constructed responses really are critical to rehearsing tasks, it can be done with powerful outcomes. Great authenticity of performance and practice can be achieved, even when only basic keyword and phrase detection is used, and even when the detection is far from perfect.

O1. Think theater. Think experience. Be dramatic. (a, b)

O2. Think role playing. (a)

O3. Provide realistic distractions and confusion. (a, b)

O5. Stay in character. (a)

O6. Make a good first impression. (a, b)

O7. Pop the challenge. (a)

O12. Create conditions—the "if"—gradually becoming more subtle from one exercise to the next. (a, b, c)

O13. To set up challenges, familiarize learners with the conditions, actions, and consequences individually. (a)

O15. Prefer controls to inputs. (b)

O16. Match controls to content and learner readiness. (a, b)

Example 5. Business Banking

As one of our bank's relationship managers (RM), you need to understand the problems and challenges our business clients face. Only then can you be of greatest assistance to them and identify services and products that could help them be successful.

I want you to experience something of what it's like to run a business. Your cash, expenses, income, profit, payables, receivables, and inventory will be reported to you as you make a series of critical decisions. It's very hard to be successful in business. Good luck!

Many RMs lack adequate knowledge of what it is really like to undertake the challenges of running a business. As a result, this simulation reverses roles. It puts RMs in the role of a business owner and challenges them to run the company, make tough decisions, experience the pain of insufficient cash flow, etc.

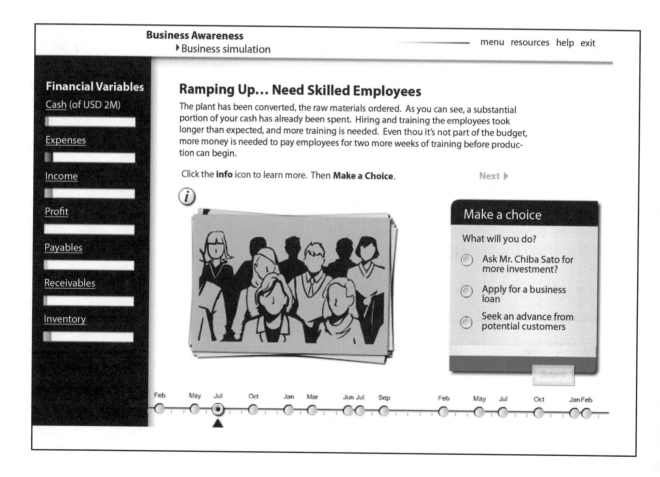

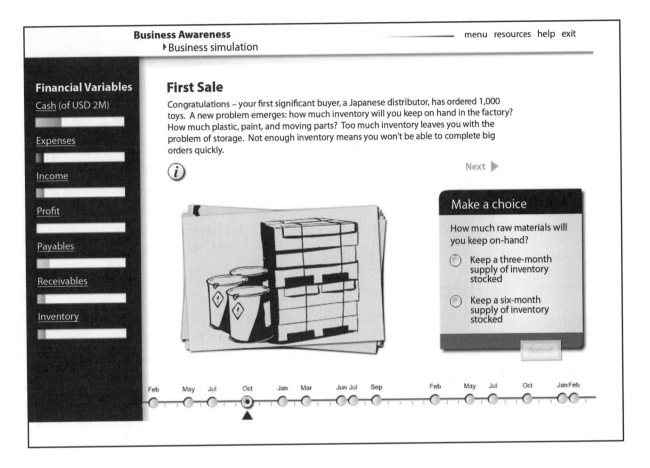

Business management is full of risks and diverse challenges. People who have never run a business often have very faulty misconceptions about it. These bank relationship managers are not being trained to run a business, but rather to empathize with the needs of their customers, to learn their viewpoints and terminology, and to become better able to suggest appropriate services as the right times.

Principles Applied
CONNECT

Roles are switched—an inherently fascinating context. Learners see their behavior from the customers' point of view. Further, learners are put in a highly responsible and powerful role of running a business with a visible list of success criteria prominently displayed on the left.

C1. Demonstrate that you know your learners. (b)

C2. Select meaningful and beneficial challenges. (a, b)

C5. Use theatrical devices. (a)

C6. Nest dramatic human consequences in the challenge. (a)

C8. The story continues. (a)

C11. Let challenges arise from learner mistakes. (a)

C13. Consequences, judgments, explanations—of these, the greatest is consequences. (a)

EMPOWER

The timeline across the bottom sequences learner choices and provides an invaluable control: learners can back up. This interface allows learners to go back in time by clicking past dates on the calendar. They can then make different decisions and witness the different outcome effects.

E2. Maintain space and place. (a, b, c, d)

E3. Make learning easier by eliminating distractions. (a)

E5. Differentiate controls from displays. (b)

E11. Empower learners with meaningful control. (b)

E12. Make control comforting and convenient. (b)

ORCHESTRATE

This single screen is home base for many interactions. The timeline provides context and orientation while introducing a series of challenges and interactions. Financial variables show the effect of each subsequent decision. Terms can be learned in context by clicking the hypertext headings on the left.

O2. Think role playing. (a, b)

O6. Make a good first impression. (b)

O7. Pop the challenge. (a)

O9. Give users options. (b)

O15. Prefer controls to inputs. (a)

O16. Match controls to learner readiness. (b)

O17. Think consequences. (a, b)

Example 6.
Shoe Store Stockroom

A kid with trendy athletic gear is browsing the shoe store's showroom. He's fidgety but carefully inspecting the merchandise. Your boss says, "I think there's a good opportunity for a sale, perhaps a large sale here. Show me how it's done."

Excellent performance often looks simple until you try to do it yourself. When on the hook, you come to realize the value of preparation. In this example, trainees need to match their observation of a possibly eclectic buyer who might easily slip away without your rapid intervention with the right mix of product alternatives. The sales person needs to know exactly where various styles are, how to keep the stock room organized for rapid product retrieval, and how to base product selection on probable customer interests.

Screen captures courtesy of Genesco, Inc.

It's important that shoe stores manage their stockrooms efficiently and consistently so that store clerks can find shoes of the correct style and size very quickly. They don't want to keep customers waiting while they are searching the stockroom, and they want to be able to find related styles as alternative or additional purchase considerations.

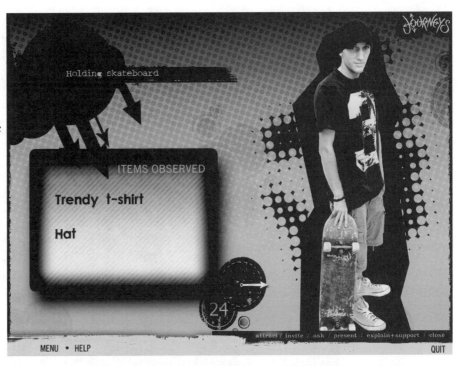

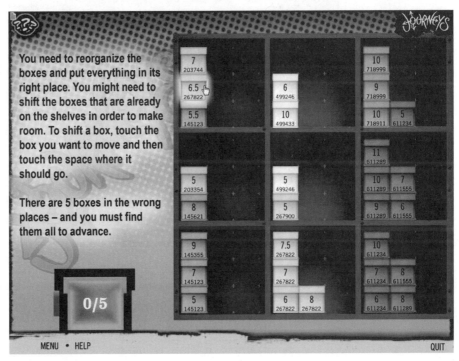

In this example, learners learn to put shoeboxes in correct places based on stock number and size. Learners must identify which boxes are misplaced and then drag them to correct positions, first moving other boxes out of the way if necessary.

Adding to the realism of the challenge, there is an irrelevant element of box color that may seem material to learners in this sorting task and can even confuse knowledgeable personnel, but is not actually the criterion for correct box placement. For example, if learners just look at box color and shoe size, they may assume that Stock # 267822–Size 6.5 belongs on the center shelf above Stock # 267900–Size 5. But actually, the box belongs on the lower center shelf, between Stock # 267822–Size 6 and Stock # 267822–Size 7.

Because being quick to sort boxes and return to the sales floor is so important, once learners demonstrate their understanding of the organizing concepts, the challenge is increased by presenting additional boxes to be placed. Additional boxes arrive on a conveyor belt so learners

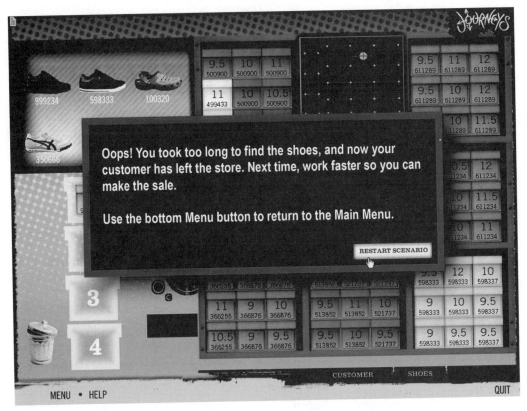

Oops! You took too long to find the shoes, and now your customer has left the store. Next time, work faster so you can make the sale.

Use the bottom Menu button to return to the Main Menu.

RESTART SCENARIO

have a limited amount of time to place each box. As skills continue to improve, shelves fill up and require more and more existing boxes to be relocated before the new ones can be placed. If learners are too slow, boxes fall off the belt and the performance score is affected.

After practicing with the conveyor belt, learners move on to serving clients. Their speed skills will be called into use. If they are too long in the stockroom, for example, learners receive a message like the one above.

Principles Applied
CONNECT

Instead of reading about why stockroom organization is so important, learners are put in situations in which they must actually use the stockroom to serve customers. They experience the whole process of organization, storing, and retrieving shoes in a visual environment that incrementally pressures learners, just as they will be pressured in job performance. Yet the whole experience exudes a game-like character that is appealing and intriguing.

C1. Demonstrate that you know your learners. (a, b)

C2. Select meaningful and beneficial challenges. (b)

C3. Activities should relate to what learners do now and will do after skill development. (a, b)

C4. It's not just what you say, but how you say it. (a)

C5. Use theatrical devices. (d)

C7. Keep the story going. (a)

C8. The story continues. (a)

C9. Context is almost everything. Choose wisely. (c)

C10. Be reasonable, but don't be a softy. (a)

C12. Don't skip over practicalities. (a, b)

C13. Consequences, judgments, explanations—of these, the greatest is consequences.

EMPOWER

The interface is extraordinarily simple. Drag boxes to their proper places. Course delivery typically occurs on touch-enabled displays. Learners are instantly empowered to perform and practice by the LID with very little preparation needed.

E1. Be visual. (a)

E2. Maintain space and place. (a, c, d)

E4. Present the challenge in the context. (a, b)

E5. Differentiate controls from displays. (a)

E6. Use contextual elements to compose feedback. (a)

E8. Build response opportunities into the context. (a, b)

E9. Integrate challenges and controls. (a)

E11. Empower learners with meaningful control. (a)

E12. Make control comforting and convenient. (b)

ORCHESTRATE

The design moves nicely from puzzle-like activity to a full simulation of serving customers. But notably, at all stages, the visual context and relevance are apparent and learner behaviors are strongly analogous to required job performance behaviors. Consequences similarly progress from not having placed shoeboxes correctly to losing customers.

O2. Think role playing. (a)

O3. Provide realistic distractions and confusion. (a, b)

O5. Stay in character. (a)

O6. Make a good first impression. (a, b)

O7. Pop the challenge. (a)

O8. Instill a sense of confidence. (a)

O12. Create conditions—the "if"—gradually becoming more subtle from one exercise to the next. (a, b, d)

O13. To set up challenges, familiarize learners with the conditions, actions, and consequences individually. (a)

O15. Prefer controls to inputs. (b)

O16. Match controls to content and learner readiness. (a, b)

O17. Think consequences. (a)

Example 7.
Travel Agent Training

A caller is on the phone, wanting to book a trip to New York City for the first time. She's checked on the Web, but is hoping for some recommendations. She's not sure where to stay and what to do while there.

As her travel agent, you have a chance to book her dream vacation. You'll also add those extra touches that will bring the caller back to you again and again. To do this, you need to learn about your caller and then use your knowledge of New York City to book that perfect trip. Ready? Go!

The use of photos, customer faces, and postcards create an immersive visual interface aligned with the intended outcomes. The screen is divided into three areas.

Screen capture courtesy of Expedia, Inc.

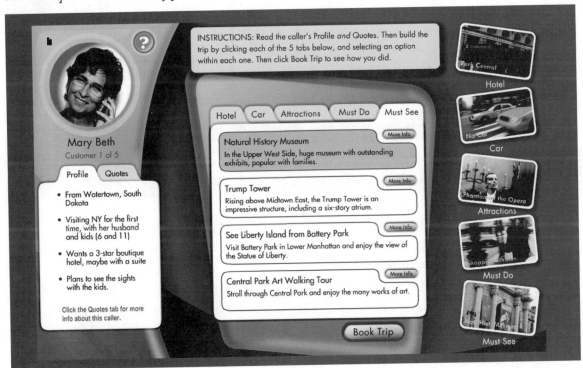

The left column provides information about the caller, taken from notes of a conversation with her. The middle column provides reservations and plans agents can make. The right column visualizes interim decisions made by the learner until the learner "books the trip."

their recommendations as often as they wish, but must eventually lock in their choices.

To personalize the experience, to underscore the personal responsibility each agent holds, and to emphasize consequences rather than judgments, feedback is provided by

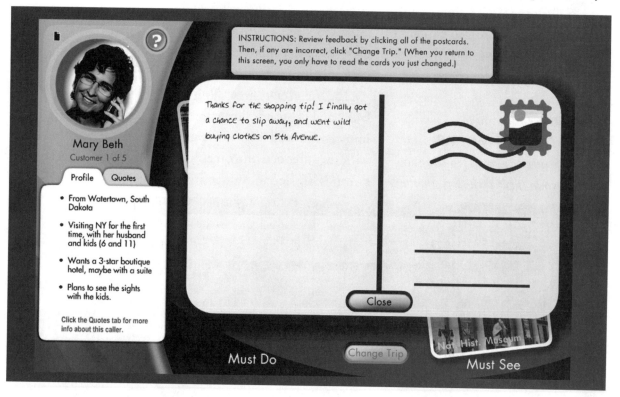

Learners can research options as much as they wish. Each learner is likely to be very familiar with some cities, moderately familiar with others, and totally unfamiliar with other cities. As learners acquire more knowledge, they are free to change

"the customer" to the travel agent through comments written on the back of postcards, one for each choice the learner made for the client. Comments can range from great appreciation, to acceptance, to severe dissatisfaction. This e-learning creates very meaningful, memorable, and motivational learning experiences.

Principles Applied
CONNECT

As usual in these high-impact examples, many CEO principles are applied, including close simulation of the job, matching activity to the objectives, providing intrinsic feedback (via the postcards), and providing contextual help and hints via customer comments. Overall, this e-learning achieves extraordinary connection with its learners and applies nearly every one of my guidelines in doing so.

C1. Demonstrate that you know your learners. (a, b, c)

C2. Select meaningful and beneficial challenges. (b)

C3. Activities should relate to what learners do now and will do after skill development. (a, b)

C4. It's not just what you say, but how you say it. (a)

C5. Use theatrical devices. (a, d)

C6. Nest dramatic human consequences in the challenge. (a)

C7. Keep the story going. (a)

C8. The story continues. (a, b)

C9. Context is almost everything. Choose wisely. (c)

C13. Consequences, judgments, explanations—of these, the greatest is consequences. (a)

EMPOWER

Learners can use readily available resources to research travel options, such as amenities and location of hotels, activities for children, types of shopping, and so on. Because agents must eventually construct a complete package, early selections, such as choice of hotels, might need to be changed as other information, such as the location of desired activities, is identified. This interface empowers learners to make initial decisions, collect additional information, and change their decisions as often as needed to create a complete package that meets all their customer's preferences.

E2. Maintain space and place. (a, c, d)

E4. Present the challenge in context. (a, b)

E5. Differentiate controls from displays. (c)

E6. Use contextual elements to compose feedback. (a)

E7. If the feedback isn't intrinsic, create a unique visual identity for it. (b)

E11. Empower learners with meaningful control. (a)
E12. Make control comforting and convenient. (a)

ORCHESTRATE

Dividing the screen into three districts, one for customer information, a second for travel information, and a third to display reservation selections, provides easy navigation for many learner activities without ever leaving the one screen. As necessary, additional information, such as postcards from customers who took trips as booked by the agent, comes into or overlays this screen. Learners can learn to operate the structure quickly, feel comfortable while doing it, and receive intrinsic feedback.

O2. Think role playing. (a)
O3. Provide realistic distractions and confusion. (a, b)
O5. Stay in character. (a)
O6. Make a good first impression. (a, b)
O7. Pop the challenge. (a)
O9. Give users options. (a)
O12. Create conditions—the "if"—gradually becoming more subtle from one exercise to the next. (b)
O15. Prefer controls to inputs. (a)
O17. Think consequences. (a, b)

I hope you've sorted out the important differences between interface designs that are appropriate for e-learning and how they contrast with designs that are appropriate for presentations, commerce Web sites, games, and general software applications. And I hope you have a sense for those elements in user interface design that are helpful to learning experiences and those that weaken them.

Let's look once again at the challenges at the end of Part One and see how your answers compare with mine. I hope you came up with better answers than mine, but if not, perhaps you'll find my perspective on these design attributes helpful.

Challenge 1

The first screen presents content from antiterrorism training and describes four primary principles first responders should use to both keep themselves safe and provide the fastest and best protective reaction.

Figure courtesy of Commission on Peace Officer Standards and Training

User Interface Design (UID)

⊙ Successful   ○ Poor

Why? From a user interface perspective, there's little functionality on the screen—few problems, not a lot to go wrong. The forward-paging NEXT button is clear. Considering the layout, the page is nicely organized, key words stand out, and there are generally no issues.

Learner Interface Design (LID)

○ Successful   ⊙ Poor

Why? This doesn't make me think. If there are many pages like this, my takeaway learning will be how fast the NEXT button responds.

Context

○ Successful   ⊙ Poor

Why? There's really no performance or emotional context here at all. This is only a presentation in lieu of a performance opportunity, using that fatal motivator, "Trust me, someday you'll be glad you know this."

Challenge

○ Successful   ◉ Poor

Why? A challenge is meant to spur the learner to action and provide means of assessing competency. While presenting text does promote reading, unless the learner faces a challenge, neither we nor the learner can know if the learner was able to extract performance guidance from the text. From an LID point of view, the challenge should come first. Text, such as this, is then available to the learner as an assist. Reading it will then be purposeful.

Activity

○ Successful   ◉ Poor

Why? Although there have been times that designers have, with a straight face, told me that a design was interactive because it had paging buttons, you won't get away with that here. There's no instructional activity present here.

Feedback

○ Successful   ◉ Poor

Why? The only feedback of any sort here is that when the next button is pressed, the page changes. This doesn't count as instructional feedback.

Compare and Contrast UI and LID

The user interface accomplishes its goal of not making me think. I almost instinctively know that I can click NEXT and move on. I would worry about doing so, but sitting there prominently, the NEXT button almost begs me to click it as soon as possible. I'd do it with hope that there would be a BACK button on the next page if it turned out I really had to remember something from this page. So from a learner interface design point of view, this page fails completely.

Challenge 2

This design presents the prescribed actions, as did Challenge 1, but not in the correct order. The learner has to think about what might be the best order in which to respond to the situation.

As a first responder to an incident, you should first:

○ **ISOLATE:** Clear the area; establish a perimeter.

○ **RECOGNIZE:** Assess from a safe distance; scan for secondary devices.

⊕ **AVOID:** Stay clear of the danger area. Your own safety comes first.

○ **NOTIFY:** Notify dispatch of all important information; request appropriate personnel; advise others of danger spots.

SUBMIT

This is the feedback that is shown if "AVOID" is chosen and is typical of other feedback messages in this design.

While you'll have to avoid dangerous areas, to do so, you need to determine where the dangers are.

Select another answer.

User Interface Design (UID)

⊙ Successful   ○ Poor

Why? As in Screen 1, there's little functionality on the screen—few problems, not a lot to go wrong. The radio buttons are a standardized and widely recognized interface device. The context and question clearly imply that only one choice can be selected. Instructions could have been added, but probably aren't needed. A rollover highlight (as shown) invites the user to click the button. Such invitations confirm expectations and contribute significantly to user comfort and confidence. Because only one answer can be selected, users can correct errors by simply clicking a preferred answer after making a mistake. The visible SUBMIT button confirms the ability to make corrections but appears inactive, as it should, until an answer is selected. The page is nicely organized, key words stand out, the text is large enough, and it contrasts well. There are generally no significant UI issues.

Learner Interface Design (LID)

○ Successful   ⊙ Poor

Why? Although the words of the question describe actions, clicking one of the choices is a completely different task from being in the moment of a crisis, complete with its dangers and distractions. Artificial tasks like this are unnecessary with the capabilities of e-learning to provide authentic tasks. This design just wastes time.

Context

○ Successful   ⊙ Poor

Why? Again there's really no performance or emotive context here to speak of. The closest it comes to providing a context is the phrase "as a first responder to an incident," but the vague notion of an incident is very weak indeed. I suspect it's more than my local Italian gelato vendor running out of pistachio, but help me out here: What are we talking about? This is a multimedia environment. Make the context vivid.

Challenge

○ Successful   ⊙ Poor

Why? This is actually quite a good question, so my rating might be a bit harsh. The question poses good alternatives and makes you think hard about the best strategy, especially if you haven't already been acquainted with the best sequence of responses to potentially dangerous situations. But an academically posed question isn't equal to an authentic challenge where learners must assess a situation, determine if action is appropriate, and then take action rather than just recognizing a correct answer in a list of alternatives.

Activity

○ Successful   ⊙ Poor

Why? Clicking off an answer from a list is very different from actually taking action. While in e-learning we're often having to substitute an approximation of an action, checking an answer is quite different from actually positioning yourself properly with respect to a suspected terrorist holdout. Technology in common use for e-learning allows us to do much better than the limited activity of selecting an answer.

Feedback

○ Successful   ⊙ Poor

Why? For the most meaningful and memorable feedback, we generally look first for the feedback to come in the form of consequences. What would be the result of choosing an incorrect answer here? Well, pretty extreme. Possibly death. Using the multimedia capabilities inherent in e-learning, feedback shouldn't come primarily in words but rather through dramatization of the consequences. Some text can, of course, be added for additional clarity and guidance.

Compare and Contrast UI and LID

This is a straightforward implementation of a multiple-choice question. If we were teaching antiterrorism teams to take multiple-choice tests, this could provide excellent practice. But we're not and this isn't.

Some might argue that clicking the first action to take should require dragging that option to the top of the list. While this user interface would be more complex, requiring the user to think more about how to enter an answer, changing the user interface wouldn't strengthen this learning event.

No, the problem isn't with the UI. It's a problem of not creating a challenge within a vivid context that allows the learner to experience the consequences of alternative actions. It's an LID problem.

Challenge 3

This screen presents an incident. "An explosion has been reported at 5th and Center Streets. Possible injuries. No further details are available at this time." Learners play the role of first responders and indicate what they would do by clicking the buttons below the scene.

Buttons present more detailed options or ask for further information. A clock times learner responses.

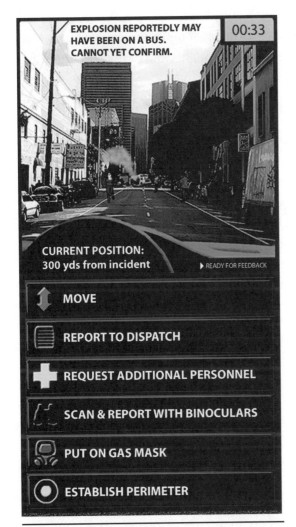

Screen capture courtesy of Commission on Peace Officer Standards and Training

User Interface Design (UID)

⊙ Successful   O Poor

Why? This is a much more complex screen, but options that are alternatives to each other are apparent. The situation is described at the top, in the brightest area of the screen, which gets my attention.

Although the clock counting elapsed time at the top is not explained, it's quite clear that it's timing my actions, and I need to avoid wasting time.

The READY FOR FEEDBACK button is related in color and shape to the primary options and communicates that I may want to do more than one thing before I indicate that I'm done. Because it appears active, it needs to be active. It could give some instruction to a user who didn't understand the implications of this screen layout and clicked this button without taking any prior actions.

Overall, this design is working.

Learner Interface Design (LID)

⊙ Successful   O Poor

Why? I feel alert and responsible. Just the fact that I "feel" something tells me this design has more power to propagate learning than the previous designs.

My options aren't generalizations; they're real actions relevant to the situation. The clock reminds me that in such situations, I wouldn't have time to break out a guidebook and look things up. I need to know this well enough to respond properly almost without thought. Practice will be important for me. I'll later appreciate tips on how to organize my thoughts and evaluate options to specific situations. Right now, I need to *think!*

Context

⊙ Successful   O Poor

Why? I'm in my car. Actually, I'm driving. I see smoke, people, and a bus ahead. I hear shouting (the audio component is a powerful aspect of this experience). When I move forward, the shouting and sound distractions grow louder. I see no other authorities around. It's clearly my responsibility to do something.

Challenge

⊙ Successful   O Poor

Why? The call to action is clear. The importance of doing things in the right order is also clear, although if I should not give sequence proper attention, the consequences will be clear and I'll do better on my next try. While recognizing a correct answer in a short list, such as that of a typical multiple-choice question, real life often presents lots of choices. It's not a matter of just recognizing the right thing to do, it's a matter of reasoning out or recalling what the right thing to do is. This design provides a nice balance and makes the situation quite authentic.

Activity

⊙ Successful   ○ Poor

Why? Of particular importance to the success of this design is that activities are done realistically. For example, scanning the situation presents a reduced breadth, but close up view through binoculars. Learners need to move the binoculars around to spot important things in the scene.

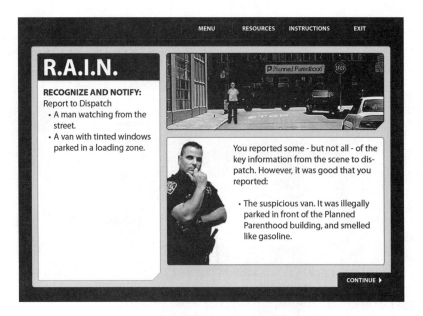

Feedback

⊙ Successful   ○ Poor

Why? Completing the set of successful LID decisions is powerful feedback. Three attributes make it particularly powerful: First, as noted above, unless the learner "dies" in the process of handling the situation, learners can make a long string of mistakes. Second, progressive feedback comes in the form of consequences. Third, undesirable consequences may be overcome if they aren't too severe, and the learner can keep working until pressing the "Ready for Feedback" button. Such delayed feedback allows learners to assess their own successes and failures. Excellent.

Compare and Contrast UI and LID

The user interface makes my options clear, and they are easy to use. But the interface doesn't preclude the necessity of my analyzing the situation and carefully selecting my action; rather, it helps me focus on my choices.

The strong context used by the LID doesn't interfere with the UI, and the UI could still be simple. Both UI and LID support a meaningful, memorable, and motivational learning experience.

Learner Interface Design Guidelines

➢ CONNECT

1. Relevance and Personalization
Viewed Through CCAF

How then do we connect with learners? Analyzing the process of connecting with learners through the CCAF lens, we can use the following guidelines for creating relevance and personalizing the e-learning experience.

Context
C1. Demonstrate that you know your learners.

C1-a). Meeting of minds. Create a context that matches the probable mindset of the audience. Do you have learners who are comfortable with reading? Are they used to solving problems on their own or as members of a team? Do they expect to see tools, machines, or instruments?

C1-b). Hero for a day. Present a situation in which each learner can easily visualize himself or herself having and managing an important responsibility—a situation that can lead to a proud success.

C1-c). Please identify yourself. If you are teaching the same content to learners who have varying skills, are on different career paths, or are likely to have different definable interests in the content and skills to be learned, provide a choice or ask a couple of questions to select a context that can be meaningful to the individual.

Challenge
C2. Select meaningful and beneficial challenges.

C2-a). Why should they care? If the role you're asking the learner to play isn't the same as the role you're asking them to play for learning, explain why it's helpful to assume the responsibilities of this role now.

C2-b). Make challenges challenging. Challenges should be neither too simple nor too difficult. Most importantly, they should require each individual to think. If prior assessment is not available to calibrate the appropriate level of challenge, try a moderate challenge at first, provide extensive help for those who happen to need it, and set the next challenge either higher or lower depending on the amount of help that was required.

Activity
C3. Activities should relate to what learners do now and will do after skill development.

C3-a). Match performance modalities. Repair technicians probably like to fix things; they like puzzles and problem solving and are visual. Don't have them write essays. Creative people hope to find that multiple solutions exist, or at least that there are multiple valid paths for arriving at solutions. Make sure they can explore options.

C3-b). True tasks. The activity should involve tasks that learners could and would actually carry out in the real world. As learners near proficiency, available support mechanisms should be reduced (or expanded) to represent those that will actually be available.

Feedback
C4. It's not just what you say, but how you say it.

C4-a). Stay in character. To personalize the experience, the feedback should be expressed in a form most meaningful and directly related to the learner. For example, rather than just showing that profits of the company dropped because of a lost sale, the company in the event story might announce layoffs as a result of poor business performance and the learner, most regrettably, is being let go. That's getting personal, huh?

2. *Humanization and Dramatic Impact*
Viewed Through CCAF

Learning experiences that connect on a human level and have dramatic impact are built from context, challenge, activity, and feedback. These components come together most dramatically and impactfully when composed and joined together by someone who personally feels and enjoys the energy and power that come from the very knowledge and skills that the learners are acquiring.

Context
C5. Use theatrical devices.

C5-a). *It was a dark and stormy night,* but the project had to be finished on time. Janice was at her wit's end without hope until you showed up. Begin a story with someone or something at risk. Put the learner in a position to help. The risk might be the possibility of not achieving an important goal or losing an opportunity, job, or something of value. Use names and create characters of interest and energize emotion. Let a storyline provide a basis for sequencing learning activities.

C5-b). Use conflict. To personalize the experience, the feedback should be expressed in a form most meaningful for and directly related to the learner. Instead, for example, of just indicating that the learner correctly communicated to passengers aboard a rocky flight, present a short video of a passenger giving emotional praise for the learner's comforting work.

C5-c). Be funny. Laughing releases endorphins that make us feel good and want more. Incorporating humor doesn't mean you aren't also serious about providing an effective use of learner time. Learners appreciate efforts to "entertrain" or "edutain" them and will respond with their attention and participation, especially if your efforts are truly entertaining as well as beneficial.

C5-d). Just (let them) do it. Avoid lengthy instruction about how to work the e-learning application. The user interface and the learner interface should be sufficiently intuitive that people can figure most of it out as they go. Tool tips and gradually revealed controls can help here. We want the context to be a content-related situation, and we do not want learners delayed getting to it. Nor do we want their focus constantly yanked away to deal with navigation or other mechanics outside the context of the experience.

Challenge
C6. Nest dramatic human consequences in the challenge.

C6-a). Solve our problem—everyone's depending on you. Challenge, activity, and feedback must all build on context to provide the best learning experience. Dramatic challenges are those with outcomes that matter. They're rarely single-step, isolated tasks. They're often provoking and complicated. Answering an academic question doesn't make the grade (sorry). But performing a procedure to meet a customer's expectations, using a software application to accomplish a task critical to a project's success, and taking proper precautions at a crime scene to protect people nearby—these can be dramatic challenges that energize learning like nothing else can.

Activity
C7. Keep the story going.

C7-a). Think real, not academic. We often break complicated tasks down into tiny steps so that learners won't be overwhelmed with a challenge that's too great for them. This is a good thing to do, but it's often done such that learners lose the sense of the context and begin performing tasks that have only artificial, abstracted, or academic consequences. We want to keep everything as authentic as possible, so even if activities have to be simplified, try to keep them within the context of the story, process, or system. Instead of having learners perform tasks they aren't yet ready to do, have learners put preceding and/or following tasks in order and click to have them performed by others so that the excitement of actually performing part of a real task is achieved.

C7-b). Face up. Inclusion of photos of people humanizes the learning space. If part of a process is performed by someone, submitted to someone, or created for someone's benefit, let's interact with faces. Ask learners to move teams together, drag a photo of a person into position to perform a task, and otherwise work with "people" rather than just letting photos of people adorn the screen (which is better than not having photos at all).

Feedback
C8. The story continues.

C8-a). Prefer consequences to judgments. Consequences that build on each other have much more dramatic impact than isolated events. Judgment tends to terminate an escalating event or chop it into segments, so be reluctant to offer judgment. Rather, demonstrate the consequences of the learner's actions continuously as the learner works to meet challenges.

C8-b). Use media to make outcomes memorable. Video from a delighted or uncontrollably angry customer will be remembered. How about audio of a caller ranting about a recently serviced car having broken down in a very remote location? Late at night! In a storm! How about a scrapbook page of a peer-aged student winning first place in a science contest with smiling teachers and parents, a tall trophy, and an ecstatic kid?

3. *Authenticity and Situational Fidelity*
Viewed Through CCAF

To fully connect with learners and help them transfer new skills to post-learning performance, it's extremely helpful to create a context, a set of challenges, and activities that represent real situations, real challenges, and the actual behavioral solutions that will work. This is situational fidelity or authenticity.

Context
C9. Context is almost everything. Choose wisely.

C9-a). It's OK to exaggerate some learning contexts for dramatic or humorous impact, but as people move closer to completing a course of learning, it's very important that the context be as authentic as possible. That is, the situations that fuel the challenges, activities, and feedback should become as similar as possible to what will really be encountered. CCAF components should be complete with their typical ambiguities, sporadic availability of resources, noise, interruptions, or whatever is typical.

C9-b). Vary contexts. When building general skills and knowledge to be transferred to many situations, it's important to provide a variety of contexts to demonstrate the wide applicability and utility of the skills being learned. Contexts should be interesting to the ages and lifestyles of the learners and also clearly show the empowerment provided by what is being learned.

C9-c). Don't play generic games. *Jeopardy* and *Wheel of Fortune* are fun games, but the context is the game itself. Using them as a learning context, as so many do, provides an authentic context only if you're preparing to be a contestant on one of these games. It's important to use a context that matches the expected arena of performance.

Challenge
C10. Be reasonable, but don't be a softy.

C10-a). Ramp up challenges. Challenges should generally be those that will actually be encountered in the context presented. While it's typical to make initial challenges unrealistically simple, it's much better to search out and use actual situations that happen to present the simpler challenges. This helps maintain fidelity, which, in turn, helps learners understand the value of what they're learning. Challenges can and should become more difficult, of course, while maintaining authenticity throughout the sequence.

C11. Let challenges arise from learner mistakes.

C11-a). Apply the domino effect. With the increasing power of our software tools, it's finally become more reasonable to let learners traverse poorly chosen paths for long enough that they can experience the consequences of their mistakes rather than just receive an immediate judgment *Sorry, that's wrong. At this point you should choose.* . . . Going just a step further, if you can, allow new challenges to arise that not only reveal a previous mistake, but give learners an opportunity to make things better (if that's possible) by meeting subsequent challenges. Since we often have opportunities in life to correct mistakes and move on, such opportunities in e-learning may represent the ultimate authenticity and situational fidelity.

Activity
C12. Don't skip over practicalities.

C12-a). If you have to do it, you have to do it. Make it necessary to actually perform steps that would be necessary. If you'd have to go to the lab to obtain supplies, call the marketing department to procure product literature, get financial data to make a presentation, or stock specific foods for your restaurant, help learners visualize the location, the means of doing these things, and the time that will be required. Of course, we would rarely want to involve all the minute steps required nor take the actual amount of time required, but being aware of these necessities and the means of accomplishing them can be important to making the experience feel real and helping the students think about the application of their learning as they are learning.

C12-b). Show it. As much as possible, make activities visual. Instead of a button labeled "fire the greenware," let learners drag unfired pottery to a kiln. To teach safety, you might actually make them set the greenware down first before they can open the kiln. You get the "picture."

Feedback
C13. Consequences, judgments, explanations—of these, the greatest is consequences.

C13-a). Be consequential. The easiest feedback is to provide learners a judgment statement. *Yes, that's correct. No, you'll need to try again.* Actually, there's an even easier one that's worse yet. For all interactions, you can give exactly the feedback regardless of response correctness: *The correct answer is _____. Click next to go on.*

The best feedback is to continually show the consequences of the learner's sequence of responses, augmented by explanation. When to give the explanation is a bit of an open question. If you give explanations at every step, you can condition learners not to think much about their choices. They'll select or input any convenient choice just to read the explanation. This short-circuits deeper thought and personal evaluation of performance, although it depends on how much and the type of explanation you give. In general, it's often better to wait until either success or irreversible failure has been achieved.

C13-b). Don't always make consequences obvious. Sometimes you have to seek feedback in real life to know what effect you're having. To make experiences authentic, you may want to require learners to take extra steps to gather data and evaluate their own performance, especially if that will be necessary in real life. Require them to click a photo of a manager and request feedback. Have them click the CFO's door to receive a financial report. Have them disassemble a product to be sure their crew assembled it properly.

C14. Consider how authentic you want to be.

C14-a). Let feedback be misleading! Yes, strange to say, but in the real world, feedback is often misleading. People want to be kind and will often tell us we're doing better than we are. Sometimes a bad decision works out well—talk about misleading feedback! Sometimes the best solution requires breaking a rule. Immediate feedback, in real life, might very well suggest we change course, but if we hang in there, we might be rewarded by superior success.

We have to cope with confusing feedback in real life and learn to cope with it effectively. If we want to be authentic and help learners cope, we'll sometimes want to introduce a similar lack of reliability in the feedback learners receive—at least the feedback that arrives in terms of consequences. If done well, by the way, true-to-life feedback can increase the level of intrigue considerably and create learning experiences that will drive water cooler discussions for months.

➤ **EMPOWER**

4. Visual Clarity
Viewed Through CCAF

Providing context, challenge, action controls, and feedback is typically done visually or at least with visual components. Much of the conversation with learners is nonverbal, even in applications dealing with language arts, as learner eyes scout out the terrain to determine what's important and what's not. Just as it's important to structure text to communicate effectively, it's important to use visual expressions well.

Context
E1. Be visual.

E1-a). Trim the text. People don't read on-screen text with accuracy. They comprehend less from on-screen text than they do from print. Use minimal amounts of text, keep the font large enough to read comfortably, and use it in support of graphics wherever possible. Better yet, skip the text and use audio to describe visuals.

E1-b). Don't fight. A red sweater stands out if the crowd isn't wearing a lot of red. But if everything is red, everything fights for attention and nothing stands out. Don't use busy backgrounds and don't put everything in busy frames; just let the primary visual objects take the honors and make everything else stand down.

E2. Maintain space and place.

E2-a). Don't erase the full screen unless you are jumping to a completely different context. Add and remove items as needed, drawing as much or little attention in the process as is appropriate. When the screen erases, learners have to reset themselves too. They have to reexamine everything on the screen to determine whether it is a new thing or something that was there before. This is a disruption; so stay put as much as possible.

E2-b). Separate out-of-context items from in-context items. Buttons for accessing help, additional examples, progress information, menus, and so on are not part of the instructional context (the bank teller's counter, the call center, the new accounting software, the hospital room). They should be set apart, probably kept in standard places, and, to maintain inertia, remain visible from event to event even when deactivated.

E2-c). Be consistent in the use of space. You increase focus, decrease distraction, and reduce effort for the learner when you establish permanent places for different types of things. However, (see next item) . . .

E2-d). Put related things together. Although keeping things in standard places helps learners know where to look for what they want, it's even more important to have related things in close proximity. Horizontal alignment is usually perceived as closer than vertical alignment (that is, put text and graphics side by side rather than one over the other).

E3. Make learning easier by eliminating distractions.

E3-a). Avoid extraneous text, graphics, animation, and audio.
Learners must focus, focus, focus. A clear to-the-point screen is far better than a pretty screen that lacks focus. Don't get cute with things that don't add meaning. You may be amused, but learners will be distracted (and probably annoyed).

E3-b). Don't box text (or other things) unnecessarily. For some reason, we seem to have a natural instinct to put text in a box. In many cases, this is unnecessary clutter and can even make text harder to read. Boxes in general take up precious space. Eliminating them often makes displays more inviting and less form-like. If you don't have a strong justification for a box or another form of divider, don't use one.

E3-c). Choose speech or text, but don't use both simultaneously. It would seem that use of two media to present the same message would provide helpful redundancy. But learners almost can't prevent themselves from comparing the two as they are presented, rather than thinking about the content. This is a distraction to be avoided. Speech has the distinct advantage of taking up no display space, but may be too fast or slow for the individual. It is difficult to select and review distinct passages, although controls can be provided to help.

Challenge
E4. Present the challenge in context.

E4-a). Speak to the learner through the context. Challenges should build on an established context (which further strengthens the context). If you're teaching customer service, let the challenge be expressed by a customer. If you're teaching automotive repair, play the concerning sounds heard when the car is started. If teaching bank fraud, show fraudulent checks.

E4-b). Use images of people. They can be pictures, drawings, or even cartoons or sketches, but humanizing the challenge makes it more personally and psychologically engaging. A short video clip of a person reporting a problem to be solved can express not only the nature of the problem but also its importance in a very clear and impressive way. In general, photographic realism has much greater impact than illustrated figures.

Activity
E5. Differentiate controls from displays.

E5-a). Allow direct manipulation of contextual objects. The screen can actually be cleaner and simpler if controls don't have to be added for moving objects. Allow repair technicians to turn knobs and flip switches directly rather than having to use a button to turn volume up, another to turn volume down, another to connect a speaker wire, and so on.

E5-b). Don't underline text unless it's a hyperlink. Not only does it look bad, but it's also a symbol for a hyperlink. Even if it is a link, you might use other means of differentiation to avoid the ghastly appearance of underscored text on the screen. Actually, how about never underlining text? Good idea.

E5-c). Give buttons and headings distinctive appearances that cannot be confused with each other. This shouldn't have to be pointed out, and yet the practice of making them look alike is perplexingly common.

E5-d). Invite action. When the mouse cursor rolls over objects that can be manipulated, visually invite action and indicate what kind of action can be taken (click, drag in one direction, etc.).

Feedback
E6. Use contextual elements to compose feedback.

E6-a). Display intrinsic feedback within context. The consequence of choices and actions is the feedback of situations and events. Learning is, in large part, becoming able to associate specific consequences with preceding situations and actions or inactions. So don't say, "Good, your mixture of hydrogen peroxide and phenyl oxalate ester will glow." Make it glow!

E7. If the feedback isn't intrinsic, create a unique visual identity for it.

E7-a). Provide mentorship in the form of an advisor. Betty Crocker, Mavis Beacon, and Aunt Jemima instilled trust in products from consumers for decades. These were fictitious personas—made-up names and images. Going as far as an avatar isn't necessary, but providing a named, pictured mentor can help learners accept and reflect on situations comfortably, while easily distinguishing between intrinsic feedback and explanatory information.

E7-b). Display judgmental feedback in a distinctive fashion, such as using an overlay with a drop shadow, a unique font and/or font color, or a unique border. The feedback should be displayed in close proximity to either the action taken, the consequences, or preferably both.

5. *Input and Control*
Viewed Through CCAF

Input and control relate mostly to the action component of CCAF, of course. But actions partner with the other components to create experiences. Let's see what learner interface designers need to consider for input and control to become most effective.

Context
E8. Build response opportunities into the context.

E8-a). Prefer direct control over remote control. For example, if a photo shows a task being performed, allow learners to click on things in the photo being done correctly (or incorrectly) rather than having to select from a remote device, such as a multiple-choice list of things in the photo.

E8-b). Make concepts, procedures, and situations tangible.
Exposition of content through text facilitates text responses, whereas visuals make the content more real and can also provide objects that learners can manipulate for more interesting response gestures and interactions.

Challenge
E9. Integrate challenges and controls.

E9-a). Use context visuals to imply the challenge and controls. For example, the image of a disassembled device with pieces randomly scattered about expresses the challenge and the controls nonverbally. Users may be uncertain about whether they need to rotate pieces to make them fit and, if so, how it is done; but with proper invitations for action, such as changing cursor shapes, learners will experiment and learn faster than through reading instructions. And they'll enjoy figuring things out more than following a set of instructions that lay it all out for them.

E10. Make challenge identification part of an action-orientated task.

E10-a). Require learners to recognize problems. Without realizing it, many learning events fail to have learners practice handling real-life scenarios because they define the problem for the learner. What may be the most critical part of successful performance is already finished and neatly served up. Present the high-level context and ask learners to probe around to determine the problem and then take steps to solve it.

Activity
E11. Empower learners with meaningful control.

E11-a). Avoid artificial restrictions. Your authoring tool or available programming skills may restrict you more than you wish, but strive not to restrict actions more than they will be restricted in real-world performance. People can typically do more than one thing at a time, so they should also do that in their e-learning experiences.

E11-b). Allow users to back up. In the real world, we can often detect mistakes we've made and correct them before someone else has to point out our errors and request correction. By delaying judgment, we're half-way there. The next task—not always an easy one to implement—is to allow learners to step back and make corrections. This rewards learners for continuously evaluating their work—an outcome we could prize.

E12. Make control comforting and convenient.

E12-a). Don't handicap learners. One of the really great things about books is that readers are in complete control. They can skip around, read sections out of order (I read magazines back to front), reread sections, highlight sections, earmark pages, and so on. Unless you have reasons to handicap learners and make their learning tasks more difficult, why not try to give learners at least the control they have over a book.

E12-b). Make controls intuitive. The thinking we want to incite should be about the content challenge. Requiring unnecessarily complicated gestures in order to respond diverts learners from productive thinking to thinking about the interface. As instructional challenges increase in difficulty, try not to make interface complexity also increase any more than necessary.

E13. Invite action.

E13-a). Signal possible actions clearly. It's important to let learners know what objects are interactive so they won't overlook input options and controls you've given them.

Feedback
E14. Make states clear.

E14-a). Communicate progress honestly. Checking off menu items or showing a progress bar is helpful to learners who need to schedule their time and meter their energy. Menus and progress bars work well if items are of similar difficulty and duration. If they're not, they can be quite inaccurate measures. Indicate relative proportions when variation is significant:

E14-b). Show the current state clearly. A design disaster found with bewildering frequency comes from confusing the display of a current state with the function of a button to change to another state.

➤ ORCHESTRATE

6. *Performance-Based Learning Objectives*
Viewed Through CCAF

Authors need to know and remember what the purpose of a learning experience is as they create it. Learners can make the best use of their experience if they monitor their own progress against a purpose and mentally project application of new facts, concepts, procedures, and skills into their workflow. The challenge then is to continually and effectively reflect and communicate the objectives through as many components of learning events as possible.

Context
O1. Think theater. Think experience. Be dramatic.

O1-a). Create tension to communicate objectives. Objectives typically have a boring, sterile, academic tone to them. Instead of listing behavioral objectives that few learners read, let the context communicate the objectives by showing a problematic situation—a disaster, layoffs, lost sale, unhappy customers, etc.

O1-b). Don't give the outcome away. Who would want to go to a movie that began by saying, "Here's what's going to happen, watch for this, and expect this outcome"? This is what many learning designs do, and this is what kills the possibility of a great and authentic learning experience.

Challenge
O2. Think role playing.

O2-a). Put the learner in the story. The objective can be very clear when you are given an assignment to perform. It makes the experience much more direct than simply learning to list the principles of good performance.

O2-b). Switch rolls. By giving learners various roles to play, they can come to understand alternate perspectives and more deeply understand dynamics or processes. For example, if you're teaching customer service, let the learners play the role of an unhappy customer. They'll actually gain a deeper sense of why learning effective skills is important.

O2-c). Let the learner mentor. Sometimes learners can be more reflective and sometimes more exploratory when another character is performing a task, subject to guidance from the learner. If the character is failing to remember and/or perform certain steps, the learner as mentor can become acutely aware of how important specific learning and performance tasks are.

Activity
O3. Provide realistic distractions and confusion.

O3-a). Make objectives real. Even though words describing situations and conditions may be there in the objective (but often aren't), *at a typical airline ticket counter,* it's easy to set aside the real-life impact of a statement about the performance environment and concentrate simply on learning how to do things. Handling a noisy environment, with frequent interruptions and constantly changing priorities may actually prove to be the toughest aspect of the learning task. Activities the learner performs must therefore encounter these same kinds of performance disruptions.

O3-b). Match activities to objectives. Although it makes sense to simplify activities for new learners so they can focus, avoid confusion, and not face overwhelming obstacles, it's easy for activity design to completely overturn critical aspects of objectives. Multiple-choice structures, for example, too often switch from an activity that should require recall or problem solving into a much simpler and unrealistic recognition activity.

Feedback
O4. Compare performance to objectives.

O4-a). Chart progress against proficiency (not content). People want to know where they are within a module or course. They often think in terms of how many more pages, chapters, or hours they have yet to go. But those measures substitute the objective of "getting through this" for the intended objective of mastery, skill-building, and competence. So chart proficiency as a measure of progress to help learners keep focused on the real objectives.

O5. Stay in character.

O5-a). Again, stay visual and authentic. Show the outcome rather than describing it, whenever possible. Will feedback in actual poor performance situations come simply as someone's neat, tidy, and respectful verbal assessment, or will people get mad? They'll probably get mad. Will an assembly line shut down? Will the sales team lose a bonus? Will the patient have months of recovery instead of days?

7. *Challenge and Help*
Viewed Through CCAF

There's no competition between presenting a challenge that's too difficult for learners and not presenting a challenge at the beginning. The up-front challenge wins. So put aside your fears and give it a try. But do it after studying the tips below so that you'll do it in an effective way.

Context
O6. Make a good first impression.

O6-a). Establish broad appeal. We may not know much about the individual yet, but learners begin sizing us up instantly. Am I going to get anything useful out of this? So, instead of starting with something bland, start with popular content in a context that has compelling components that are easy to relate to.

O6-b). Get into it quickly. Look for an initial context and challenge that are easy to grasp. There are so many ways to delay getting learners active, and all of them risk putting learners into a passive mode. So, especially at the outset, try for a context and challenge that don't require extensive explanation.

Challenge
O7. Pop the challenge.

O7-a). Ready, fire, aim. While it's not always a good strategy to "just do something," it's definitely not a good idea to delay putting the challenge on the table. Don't precede the challenge with lots of orientation, instructions, qualifiers, or other detail, even if you have to go back later to provide more details about the context upon which the challenge is based.

O8. Instill a sense of confidence.

O8-a). Not too easy or too hard. Too easy is better than too hard, but getting it about right is best. There is leeway and, by supplying proper help and feedback, you can move all learners comfortably through initial challenges until you can adjust the challenge level so that less exhaustive support is necessary.

O8-b). Provide a worked example. Worked examples have shown exceptional instructional power, but unless learners have a problem of their own to work, reviewing worked examples can be yet another way of delaying activity and putting learners in a passive mode. So go ahead and present the challenge, but provide access to one or more similar reference challenges together with step-by-step explanations of their solutions.

O8-c). Be ready with graduated help. But don't help too much. This may be the trickiest part. You want to respond to the learner's request for help, but you don't want to provide a shortcut that makes thinking unnecessary. If it's true that the purpose of human life is to find the shortest path between any two points, it's true that learners will take the easiest path they can find. If it's to request help because help reveals answers easily, learners will request help without facing your challenges at all. One solution is to give only hints rather than answers. Going further, you can require learners to make effortful attempts to answer after receiving each hint before another will be offered, thus making it easier to actually attempt solutions rather than to repeatedly request help.

O8-d). Mix levels. Don't continually make challenges harder. Mix in some easier ones for practice and review, including some really easy ones just to remind learners how much progress they've made. Mixing challenge levels increases fun and interest.

O8-e). Power up. The strengths that learners acquire should empower them. At some point, reward progress by giving achievers extra capabilities, such as auto completion of simple or preparatory tasks that have been thoroughly mastered. Learners will appreciate being given partial solutions and find them very rewarding.

O8-f). Offer control. It's rewarding and motivating to be given the reins, to be allowed to steer. As learners progress, consider giving them more and more control. It's perhaps a form of "power up," but control can include such options as deciding for yourself whether to practice more now and push for progress later or try moving up right away and practice later.

Activity
O9. Give users options.

O9-a). Allow "studying up." Concurrent with giving learners challenges they may not be prepared to meet, it's important to provide effective and reassuring support. It's smart to avoid the tradition of explaining everything to learners first and asking them to understand and remember it all until they finally apply it. But that doesn't mean you should intentionally withhold information. Have good help, such as demonstrations, guides, worked examples, and full reference documentation, available for when learners ask for it. Allow learners to pause interactions without penalty in order to study.

O9-b). Allow "do-overs." We've observed that with many of our best-designed interactions, learners want the opportunity to do them over. Why? Because, quite commonly, in the first "do-over" learners want to confirm for themselves that they can do much better, if not perfectly. In the second "do-over" (yes, forget that simplistic and erroneous notion that learners want and will only accept 5-to-15-minute learning sessions; they may suffer poor designs for only a very short time, but with good ones, learners aren't always looking for a quick exit), learners will do something very, very smart:

They will intentionally experiment with wrong answers to see what happens. This exploration can yield many great learning moments.

O9-c). Allow previewing. Who doesn't skim through a book to get a sense of its contents, length, and style? Even online booksellers have found it important to allow buyers to browse through books before purchasing.

O10. Provide assistance.

O10-a). Be there. Although you can't physically be there for learners, your presence can be felt if you provide support and help. As learners work to meet challenges, sense when help is needed and offer it. Think about offering help after a string of poor responses, frequent use of links to reference materials without interleaved correct responses, long delays between responses, and so on.

O10-b). Don't penalize use of help. In many contexts, asking for help requires taking some risk. *Does it reveal that I'm not prepared or paying attention? Maybe I shouldn't admit I'm confused. It might go on my record.* Unless it's a certification or evaluation exercise, we want learners to ask for help. Don't penalize them for doing so. However, (see next point) . . . .

Feedback
O11. Provide "power up" tips.

O11-a). Be a generous tipper. Because we don't want to expound content before learners become active and because we want intrinsic feedback to reveal results of learner activities, we have limited opportunities to provide tips and ancillary information. When learners ask for information or flounder, there's no problem. We can always provide additional information when requested. But if learners succeed without such help, don't forget to tip anyway: speak up at the point of transition from one event to another, providing learners the opportunity to replay the previous challenge and test out the advantages of your tips. Explanations can round out learners' knowledge and help them understand why certain behaviors produce results they want.

O11-b). Don't give away too much. Just as help can yield so much information that learners can figuratively or even literally cut and paste answers without thinking, feedback can do the same thing. In some designs, learners can enter any random response to receive feedback that eventually reveals the correct answer. So that's what learners do.

8. *Performance-Relevant Input and Control*
Viewed Through CCAF

A primary purpose of learner input capabilities and controls is to help people experiment with condition-action-consequence relationships, learn them, and apply them. Undertaking from this perspective content analysis prepares you to create your contexts, challenges, activities, and feedback. It gives you an excellent foundation for orchestrating your learning events.

Context
O12. Create conditions with the "if" gradually becoming more subtle from one exercise to the next.

O12-a). Elementary, my dear Watson. Scrutinizing the context for the critical "if" conditions is almost always the first step toward successful performance. Learners need to become skilled in recognizing the conditions—a learning and performance objective that's often overlooked. At first, conditions should be clear so learners can identify them. But as skills develop, they should become less obvious to provide practice on investigating conditions.

O12-b). Match media to real-world sources. If some information is available only in spreadsheets, in charts, in textual documents, through discussion or other forms of communication and resources, select media that most directly match the sources learners will need to use.

O12-c). Hide what's hidden. If real performance contexts have information that must be sought out, extracted, or constructed, and learners will actually have to do this to perform well, we want them practicing these skills in their e-learning. So if critical information is often hidden, require learners to take steps to uncover it, to ask necessary questions, or even fill out requisition forms.

O12-d). Facilitate multiple challenges. It takes time to become familiar with a context. If just one context can host multiple problems and performance conditions, learners will be able to get more practice from a less costly e-learning application.

O12-e). Invite alternative actions. There's little to be learned from a context that puts forth only one condition the learner can respond to. Set up multiple conditions with multiple possible actions.

O12-f). Supply incorrect information. If it happens that information is sometimes incorrect and it's important to corroborate information before acting, provide incorrect information without being obvious about it. Give learners realistic means of validating information.

Challenge
O13. To set up challenges, familiarize learners with the conditions, actions, and consequences individually.

O13-a). Challenge learners to observe conditions. Before learners can associate specific conditions with appropriate actions, they need to know what to look for. Have them demonstrate and/or build their abilities to discern salient aspects of conditions—even guessing if they need to.

O13-b). Familiarize learners with actions to consider. Learners need to have an idea of actions that are possible. They may not be able to guess what's possible or, at the opposite extreme, you may not be able to list all the actions that should be considered. Providing examples and clarifying whether there are either correct actions to memorize or a reference procedure to use will help prepare learners for their challenges.

O13-c). Don't give away consequences. Doing so can be like reading the last chapter of a mystery novel first. Don't take the experience out of the experience by foreshadowing consequences of alternative actions the learner can choose. You will want to state goals, such as "find the accounting error," "assign tasks to the best individuals to handle them," or "make sure the customer is satisfied before concluding the call." But don't indicate the consequences of either good or poor performance in any detail. That will reduce the impact of the subsequent consequences and feedback.

O14. Associate conditions and actions with consequences.

O14-a). Forward association. Although we don't want to spoil the power of intrinsic feedback, it can be a powerful exercise for learners to think ahead about possible consequences. Ask learners to predict what consequences would happen if they took various actions.

O14-b). Backward association. Create challenges that ask learners to explain what actions would have resulted in different consequences.

Activity
O15. Prefer controls to inputs.

O15-a). Invite exploration. Because we're always trying to prepare learners to do valuable things, we want them busy doing things frequently in their e-learning experiences. Invite learners to be curious and adventurous. Let them become acquainted with their learning environment through exploration rather than through your painstakingly thorough explanation of everything.

O15-b). Match behavioral modalities. If the real-world activity would require moving something, have learners drag objects. If they would have to type a message, have them type one. If they'd have to tell a caller his credit application is being denied, have them record what they would say. If they'd circle a point on a map, have them circle a point on a map. Try not to make activities either more complicated or less complicated than actual performance will require, keeping in mind that you may want to start with simplified activities and build up to greater fidelity. (See O16-b on learner readiness below.)

O16. Match controls.

O16-a). Match controls to content. Consider the nature of the content when selecting activity modalities. Sometimes the content necessitates activity modalities that don't really represent actions learners will perform. To learn where to place seismographic equipment, for example, it's not necessary to simulate driving a truck from location to location to place seismographs. Moving icons on a map is a much better modality match.

O16-b). Match controls to learner readiness. For complex tasks, things may need to be simplified at first. Almost everything is a candidate for simplification. Conditions can be made much simpler than any that will really be found, the choice of actions can be both restricted and presented as a list of choices that would never actually be provided, and the controls and inputs can be simplified so that learners have fewer things to learn all at once. As learner capabilities develop, controls can become more complex and realistic to aid with transfer of learning to real-world performance.

Feedback
O17. Think consequences.

O17-a). Use intrinsic feedback. Consequences are intrinsic feedback and much more impactful than giving learners extrinsic feedback. (*Yes, that's correct!*) Showing learners what has happened because of their actions helps cement the relationships among conditions, actions, and consequences.

O17-b). Delay judgment. It's not unusual that those consequences in life that reveal the quality of our action are delayed. Meaningful consequences often don't appear until we've completed a series of actions. In many cases, parroting this real-life experience makes e-learning experiences more effective. Delays not only teach learners that they won't always receive immediate feedback, but they also encourage learners to continuously evaluate their work and scurry around to make corrections if necessary while there may still be time.

O18. Provide mentorship.

O18-a). Check first steps. Did the learner not understand the conditions set forth in the context? In helping learners build the condition—action—consequence associations, it's important to make sure learners didn't misread the conditions and set off on the wrong path, take the wrong actions, and obtain baffling consequences. If they did go off on a tangent because of misreading conditions, provide explanation and hold their hands as you step through the solution, starting with context analysis.

O18-b). Prompt beginning learners. Provide observations and assistance, perhaps through representation of a coach. Do it without giving away answers, which can cause learners to lean heavily on the coach and avoid developing independent skills. Remind learners of things to consider—not just the things they haven't considered, but a mix of both those they appear to have remembered and not remembered.

O18-c). Promote exploration and initiative. Keeping experiences interesting and realistic requires some dependency on learner curiosity and willingness to explore. If learners haven't exercised controls that would be helpful, haven't tapped resources (hidden or in plain sight), or otherwise been effective in use of your learning affordances, some helpful prompts can make the experience much more effective. But avoid the temptation to "explain every cotton-pickin' thing" solution. It's very easy to get boring (and you know you'll want to do it). Don't.

➤ MISCELLANEOUS GUIDELINES

To help, the following is an unordered list of miscellaneous design principles to consider. Many fall into the category of user interface design principles rather than uniquely learner interface design (LID) principles and are therefore not covered in-depth elsewhere in this book, but they impinge on LID and are therefore important to consider.

M1. Differentiate Active and Inactive Elements

It seems obvious, manifest, inviolable. One should not (1) run over pedestrians, (2) put poisons on the spice rack, or (3) make active and inactive screen elements look alike.

M2. Stay Put

Good screen design is difficult. No doubt about it. Each screen layout presents unique challenges, but you can move things around a bit to accommodate the specific contents of each page. Different background, border, or font colors might look better with different content elements. It's easy to make these changes with today's software. *But don't!* Stick with one or just a small number of basic screen layouts, carrying them forward from one interactive instance to another. The framework will become a recognized context that helps learners understand which rules of engagement are in effect without having to continually reassess the situation. Consistency helps learners notice exactly what has changed and thus should not be overlooked. If everything has changed in appearance, learners must assess everything to see what has changed in substance.

M3. Avoid Erasing the Screen

Positive screen inertia is pretty much destroyed when the screen is completely erased. Our confidence that we know what is and is not in the space becomes uncertain. Even if what appears after the erasure seems just like the screen on display a second ago, we instinctively and appropriately begin a search to see whether anything changed. If anything has changed, every future screen erasure is also a signal to learners that they should carefully review the entire layout before going on, wasting precious attention span.

M4. Use Interface Conventions Consistently

This is yet another common practice that shouldn't have to be mentioned. Mixing conventions seems so obviously detrimental. But it occurs with alarming frequency.

M5. Don't Crowd the Screen

White space is important. When designers refer to white space, they actually mean the empty space used to separate items and to help draw attention to important elements. White space doesn't have to be white, although white and black are often good color choices for open space. It can be any color—even a subtle gradient or pattern. The background should contrast strongly with other display elements and allow the eye to focus comfortably on display elements without distraction.

M6. Present Text Effectively

Remember always, people don't like reading text on the screen and, what they do read, they read with reduced comprehension. Learners generally want and expect action-based encounters when using a computer.

M7. Use a Small Color Palette Purposefully

There are lots of colors to choose from. Hundreds, thousands, millions. The more the better, right? No. Almost the reverse.

Color has learning value only when it (1) systematically highlights, groups, or classifies selected objects (that is, the color has meaning), (2) creates helpful realism, or (3) enhances focus, clarity, and legibility. Displaying many colors at one time makes none of them valuable; they just fight with each other for attention with none winning. Too many colors: none of them have much impact. Inconsistent use of color: noisy, confused message. No meaningful use of color: missed opportunity.

M8. Use a Small Number of Fonts Purposefully

Oh, please! Don't use a plethora of fonts just because they're there, because you like each one of them, because it's possible, or for any other reason. We are not writing ransom notes or creating walls of graffiti. A jumble of fonts makes reading screen text even more difficult and unpleasant than it normally is. Severely restrict the number of fonts you use. Just as with the application of colors, change fonts only when there is a clear reason to do so. Define your rules for usage and stick with them.

M9. Go on an Eye Candy Diet

Yet another type of distraction that happens primarily, I suppose, because it has become possible, is extravagant visual adornment. Glitz. Eye candy. Pretty. Fun. But, like chocolate caramel ice cream sundaes, it's bad for you.

M10. Feature Learning Activities, Not Navigation

Navigation capabilities are important for most learning applications, but they are in many ways like a picture frame. They need to be supportive but not in competition for the viewer's attention. Some navigation systems are distracting simply because of the strength of their graphic design. It is often easy to justify the extra time and effort to embellish navigation components because they are used repeatedly throughout an application. But the resulting visual refinement of navigation elements can draw attention away from the sometimes plain appearance of content.

M11. Maintain Focus

Ever look at a screen and wonder which of all the things there you should be attending to? It happens when the visual space is unfamiliar or loaded with complexity. With all the interactive and informative elements we can provide simultaneously, it becomes all too easy to overwhelm learners. Valuable techniques that help learners focus on the right things include spatial placement, grouping, animation, and contrast.

M12. Keep Navigation in Its Place

Two seemingly opposite approaches help differentiate navigation from content and keep focus on the content: fixed screen divisions and floating navigation panels.

Fixed divisions. Anchoring navigation into a space continuously reserved for it is often best. Once learners become accustomed to the navigation structures, they develop an ability to see past them and ignore them almost completely except when they need to select a feature. It's what psychologists call accommodation, and it occurs when a stimulus becomes so familiar that it no longer draws our attention. Animation and sound effects can override accommodation and bring special attention to navigation components when needed. Otherwise, the navigation sits quietly; it's helpful but transparent.

Floating panels. Sometimes the entire screen is needed for content components, such as when simulating a software application or operating system that normally commands the whole screen. In this situation, layering the screen can provide both screen division and the ability to see all areas. The navigation panel should be designed to contrast with but not upstage information displays. It should be easy to move, because the learner may have to take an active role in moving the panel out of the way if the software can't find a reliable basis for doing it automatically.

M13. Group Visual Elements

There is a tendency to put too much information on the screen at one time. Indeed, even with today's high-resolution color displays, it's a challenge to effectively present as much information as can be done well on a printed page. It is very easy to overload or dazzle the learner with too many displayed content items, interactivity options, and navigation controls. Still, context is important, and dispensing with it isn't a good solution to a clutter problem. It obviously wouldn't do to present a graphic on one screen followed by its description on the next and questions about it on the next. Interactivity designers are constantly grappling with the need to make the most effective use of the space.

M14. Animate for a Purpose

Just as unique or out-of-place things draw our attention, we are also predisposed to look at moving objects. Content can be animated in attention-getting ways that really help draw our attention.

M15. Use Contrasts to Communicate More Clearly

Contrast exists in size, position, texture, scale, animation, volume, timbre, saturation, transparency, and color. In general, our attention is drawn to things that are different—that contrast with others.
A good rule for contrast, whether it's color, text size, or any other parameter: If two items aren't the same, make sure learners can easily discern the difference. Subtle differences can be attractive, but they often confuse functionality. So make contrasts big and bold.

M16. Make Text Legible

Why wouldn't you? Don't know. But so often I see text that's very hard to read. Be alert for illegible text. Some examples:

> ➢ Red text on a blue background (or vice versa) doesn't work. Your eye can't focus well on these two colors simultaneously.

> ➢ Not all learners will have great vision, so keep text larger than necessary for people with average vision.

➢ Don't put small or lightweight text over photos or illustrations that have varied colors or textures. It can be impossible to read and looks bad.

M17. Sound Off

Sounds add a strong dimension to interactive applications. Just as with color and animation, however, sounds have as much ability to be distracting and annoying as they do to be helpful and pleasing.

M18. Invite Gestures—Static Invitations

You can simplify mouse-driven interactions by highlighting click- and rollover-sensitive objects or distinguishing them in some other consistent manner (color or grouping, for example), thereby inviting learners to consider using these interactive objects and informing them of the gestures that will be recognized. We should use different indications for click, rollover, or drag activation or any other activating gesture. Invitations might take the form of a surrounding glow, a drop shadow, a bright color, underlining, 3D perspective, alignment in a banner, and so on, as long as the use is consistent. Using standards found frequently in other applications or the Internet reduces learning time and trial-and-error mistakes.

M19. Invite Gestures—Dynamic Invitations

The message that an object is active should be confirmed by, for example, a highlight that appears when the mouse pointer rolls over the object. Rollovers need only indicate that they have been activated with the pointer over them, whereas click, double-click, and drag gestures may need to be invited with a second-level invitation such as a change in the pointer's shape.

M20. Rollover and Play Alive

There is something pleasing about making something happen simply by moving the pointer over an object. Nearly effortless retrieval of helpful information can be an excellent aid for thinking and an outstanding capability of e-learning. But rollovers aren't universally applicable. Designers need to be careful with them.

M21. Double Your Clicks; Double Your Frustration

Clicking an object to select it becomes very natural for frequent computer users, but for some, clicking an object takes a bit of mental adjustment and fortitude, especially when a click sometimes initiates action and other times harmlessly selects an object for future action. It's extremely important for applications to respond consistently to every click. If one item opens with a single click, but other items open only with a double click, significant confusion and anxiety can build. Truly, one little design slip and learners feel they can't trust your interface.

M22. Minimize Drag-and-Drop Woes

If double-clicking is an obstacle for learners, drag-and-drop gestures can be almost impossible for them. It's unfortunate, because there are times when this gesture seems very appropriate for the skill being taught.

M23. Consider Click-to-Place Instead of Drag-and-Drop

A simpler interface that can often substitute for drag-and-drop interactions is click-to-place. The learner first clicks an object to be placed. The object highlights. The learner then clicks a desired location and the object is animated into the clicked location. No dragging or complex highlighting is involved.

M24. Don't Start from Scratch

There are two layers of navigation and interface features that are almost always required in e-learning applications. The top layer includes features for topic selection, overview access, progress recall, quit, and resume. Context- and content-specific features provide the second layer, including support for entering and editing responses, controlling simulations, and accessing related resource information and help.

Experienced designers know how to handle these structures and rarely start completely from scratch. It is quite effective and expeditious to adapt previous designs that have proven successful and flexible.

M25. Let Others Judge

There are, in fact, many learner interface design solutions known to experienced design teams, but even experts do some pretty horrendous things. Interface designers rarely have much trouble using their own interfaces, so they often conclude too easily that their designs are intuitive and user-friendly for everyone. Thankfully, it doesn't really take an expert to judge whether an interface is easy to use. It does, however, take some objective evaluation and some open-mindedness.

M26. Plan for More

Experienced designers know that more controls and interface features than initially expected will be desired and probably added. In their prototypes, they are careful to both reserve space and to delay refinement of global interface protocols until the desired learning experiences have taken clear shape.

Index

Challenges: antiterrorism training use of, 5, 169; authenticity/situational fidelity, 62–63; CCAF for viewing help and, 20, 94–98; connecting through, 55, 58, 62–63; context used to facilitate multiple, 101; first responder training, 5, 7, 10, 171, 174; getting over fear of presenting, 93–94; humanization/ dramatic impact through, 58; input and controls through, 78–79; interactive learning events, 33–36; performance-based learning objectives through, 91; performance-relevant input and control through, 102; poor versus good, 34–36; relevance through, 33–34; relevance/personalization through, 55; visual clarity through, 74. See also CCAF

Challenging learners, 26

Chemistry 101 (Wilbur College), 47

Child learning experience, 85–86

Click-to-place, 139

Clicking/double-clicking, 137

Cognitive activity, 40–41

Color display: contrast used for, 133; purposeful use of, 126

Commission on Peace Officer Standards and Training, 150, 167, 173

Concepts (tangible), 77–78

Conditions: associate consequences and, 102; challenges to familiarize learners with, 102; "if," 100

Conflict, 57–58

Connection/connecting: activity for, 55, 58–59, 63; attention required for, 47–49; authenticity and situational fidelity for, 24, 50, 60–65; Business Banking application of, 157–158; challenges for, 55, 58, 62–63; context for, 50, 54, 57–58, 61–62; Corrective Lenses—Optics application of, 145–146; feedback for, 55–56, 59–60, 63–65; functional, 49–51; human-

ization and dramatic impact for, 24, 50, 56–60; Infant/Toddler Safety Hazards application of, 149; introduced as CEO component, 23–24; Police Officer Training I application of, 151; Police Officer Training II application of, 154; relevance and personalization for, 24, 50, 51–56; Shoe Store Stockroom application of, 161–162; Travel Agent Training application of, 165

Consequences: associate conditions and, 102; connecting actions to, 99–100, 102; delayed judgment or, 104; don't always make them obvious, 64, 102; as intrinsic feedback, 104; providing, 63–64. See also Actions

Content: as key to relevance/personalization, 52–56; learning events organized around, 56; match controls to, 103; performance-based learning objectives through, 91

Content-unique design requirements, 114

Context techniques: avoiding extraneous text, 72; be funny, 58; build response opportunities into context, 77–78; consistent in use of space, 72; create tension to communicate objectives, 91; creating "if" conditions, 100; don't box text unnecessarily, 73; don't erase the full screen, 71–72; don't fight, 71; don't give the outcome away, 91; don't play generic games, 61–62; eliminating distractions, 72–73; facilitating multiple challenges, 101; hero for a day, 54; hide what's hidden, 100–101; invite alternative actions, 101; it's OK to exaggerate, 61; just (let them) do it, 58; make good first impression, 94; matching media to real-world sources, 100; meeting of minds, 54; please identify yourself, 54; prefer direct control over remote control, 77; put related things together, 72; separate out-of-context items from in-context items, 72; supply incorrect information, 101; trim the text,

Q

R

S

T

trimming the, 71

Text/narration triad, 69

3 M's guidelines: on audio and sound, 133–134; avoid erasing the screen, 124; click-to-place, 139; clicking/double-clicking, 137; differentiate active and inactive elements, 123; don't crowd the screen, 125; don't start from scratch, 139–140; drag-and-drop, 80–81, 137–139; feature learning activities not navigation, 128–129; go on a eye candy diet, 128; group visual elements, 130–132; invite gestures—dynamic invitations, 135; invite gestures—static invitations, 134–135; letting others judge the design, 140–141; maintain focus, 129; make text legible, 133; present text effectively, 125–126; reserving space for more refinements to design, 141; rollover and play alive, 135–136; stay put, 124; use contrast to communicate more clearly, 133; use interface conventions consistently, 124–125; use a small color palette purposefully, 126; use small number of fonts purposefully, 127

3 M's (meaningful, memorable, motivational): introduction to, 18–19; miscellaneous guidelines for, 123–139; procedural guidelines for, 139–141

Timelines (interactive), 53

Tollet, J., 127

Travel Agent Training example: background information on, 163–165; Connect principle applied to, 165; Empower principle applied to, 165–166; Orchestrate principle applied to, 166

Tufte, E., 109–110

Typeface, 127

U

User interface design (UID): comparing LID antiterrorism training and, 3–8, 167–169; comparing LID first responder to explosion training and, 9–13, 173–176; comparing LID mental involvement and, 16; inviting action using drag and drop, 80–81; minimizing the attention/effort of learners challenge of, 17–19; transparency and ease of use aims of, 23. See also Interface design

V

Visual clarity: activity for, 74–75; CCAF for viewing, 71–75; challenge for, 74; context for, 71–73; empowering by designing, 25, 70; feedback for, 75; understanding importance of, 70–71

W

Watch Mr. Wizard (TV show), 21, 22, 24, 25, 57. See also Mr. Wizard Studios, Inc.

Web design: caution when applied to e-learning, 113; information access in, 112; issues to consider for, 112; user direction element of, 112–113. See also Application design; Presentation design

Weight management training, 105

"What's the Secret?" (interactive series), 87

Wheel of Fortune (TV quiz game), 31, 61

Wilbur College, 47

Williams, R., 127

Z

Zebra technology, 69

About Allen Interactions Inc.

Allen Interactions was formed by learning technology pioneers who have continuously created precedent-setting learning solutions since the late 1960s. Their award-winning custom design and development services have been commissioned by Apple, American Express, Bank of America, Boston Scientific, Comcast, Delta Air Lines, Disney, Ecolab, Essilor, Hilton, HSBC, IBM, Medtronic, Merck, Microsoft, Motorola, Nextel, UPS, Travelocity, and hundreds of other leading corporations.

Working with IBM and then with Control Data Corporation, Michael Allen led the development of the first two widely used LMS systems. Then his pioneering work on visual authoring systems led to the ground-breaking Authorware, which elevated the level of interactivity that educators could develop and saw the creation of Macromedia, which delivered a powerful collection of interactive multimedia tools.

Now, his studios at Allen Interactions carry on the search for more meaningful, memorable, and motivational instructional paradigms, faster and lower-cost methods of designing and building technology-enhanced learning solutions, and ways to share their discoveries with those interested in more effective learning. Widely recognized as the foremost company in e-learning, Allen Interactions provides a wide range of consulting and training services, tools and software, and custom-learning design and development. They can be contacted at alleninteractions.com or by phone at 651-203-3700.

About the Author

Starting his work in technology-enhanced learning at Cornell College in the late 1960s, Michael W. Allen has been developing instructional paradigms, systems, and innovative tools ever since. He holds M.A. and Ph.D. degrees in educational psychology from The Ohio State University and is an adjunct associate professor at the University of Minnesota Medical School in the Department of Family Medicine and Community Health.

Active in e-learning organizations, publishing, and speaking, he has consulted internationally with governments and major corporations on the use of technology for learning over a period of decades. He was director of R&D for advanced educational systems within the PLATO and artificial intelligence groups at Control Data. He created the first commercial LMS products used internationally; the precedent-setting visual authoring tool, Authorware; and countless instructional applications. His first book, *Michael Allen's Guide to e-Learning: Building Interactive, Fun, and Effective Learning Programs for Any Company*, has been praised by beginners and experts alike and is the base text for ASTD's e-learning design certificate programs and many other courses of instruction around the world. *Michael Allen's e-Learning Annuals* have been noted as a "phenomenal resource" for scholars and practitioners alike, carrying up-to-date controversies and conversations from renowned experts.